Hacking the Human II
The Adventures of a Social Engineer

by
Ian Mann

A CIP record for this book
is available from the British Library

ISBN 978-0-9573809-9-8

Contents

PART TWO
The New Subconscious

Introduction

This morning, the information security manager of a large multinational arrived at work. After going through the usual site security routines, he headed for his office. He placed his key in the door and turned it, but the key didn't move as far as he expected. He realised the door was already open. Strange, as he was sure he had locked it the night before. Entering, he found my colleague and myself already sitting at his small meeting table, having gained unauthorised access to the site, ready to greet him.

We like to give regular feedback on progress, and waiting in his office was a nice touch.

So how did we gain access to this site, defeating the security entry controls?

As a social engineer, my job is to highlight security vulnerabilities connected with people, so physically breaking in isn't an option. I need to trick my way in.

My role is to analyse systems and find security vulnerabilities. Testing is then usually a good way to illustrate what is possible, and help focus the minds of management into taking remedial action.

In this case, I actually went straight up to reception as a visitor. I had completed a previous security test at this facility, and managed to bypass reception using a few different techniques. On this test, I wanted to directly trick reception into giving me access.

It was just before 9 a.m.:

"Good morning. I'm here to see Shaun Wakefield."

It's a simple request that the young lady at reception will receive many times each day. However, today something was different. She typed the name into her system, but couldn't find a Shaun Wakefield. I expect this, as it is actually the name of my colleague, who was entering the site through a different route.

"I can't seem to find Mr Wakefield on the system", she said, looking slightly puzzled.

"That's fine. Shaun is new", I responded.

"I've just spoken to him on his mobile. He's on his way, and will meet me here, so you can issue me a pass."

"Okay, can you spell your name for me, please?"

I proceeded to spell my name, and then Shaun's, so that she could issue me with a visitor pass for the day. On this site, it was the norm to give visitors a proximity access card to get through the barriers. The security is based on the fact that an employee has to be contacted and comes to collect the visitor. I had just compromised this system by using a name that is not on the system.

Therefore, I now had my access card, and the only challenge was that the receptionist thought I was to be collected.

However, a combination of the layout of reception and my timing (the busy period first thing in the morning) means that I could simply slip into the site whilst the receptionist was distracted.

A nice start to the day, and another vulnerability uncovered for our client.

At one level, this might appear to be quite a simple attack. But there is more to social engineering than just spotting a weakness and acting a part.

Having done previous tests for this client, I knew that security procedures had been improved, and training given to staff. The 'strict' process was to locate the member of staff from the system and contact them – how could I bypass this? My solution was to deliberately break the system with a name that would not be recognised.

You might think that creating an unusual situation would just alert someone to the intrusion. Actually, it can have the opposite effect. The receptionist did not expect this situation, and therefore didn't know what to do. When someone feels a bit lost, they look for a solution. As a social engineer, my job is to supply the solution for them. My words were carefully chosen:

"That's fine.... is used to reassure her that the situation is actually okay.

"....you can issue me a pass" is actually an instruction to the subconscious.

Welcome to my world of social engineering, on day one of a scheduled testing project.

2008 saw the publication of *Hacking the Human - Social Engineering Techniques and Security Countermeasures*. It was the culmination of four years of work, fuelled partly by my testing and consulting work within ECSC Ltd, and also the result of extensive research into human psychology.

At the time, there was only one other book published on the subject, and nothing available that explored the underlying psychology that leads to these information security-related human vulnerabilities.

Within *Hacking the Human*, I defined social engineering as follows:

'To manipulate people to trick them into giving out information, or performing an action'.

Now, nearly five years since publication, this definition still stands up, and is useful as a context for this book.

I must personally thank all the reviewers, both online and within security publications, who received *Hacking the Human* with such enthusiasm. When an information security manager of a major financial institution tells me it is "the best security book I have ever read", or a respected information security academic tells me, "it's changed the way I think about security", the many evenings spent on my consulting travels re-drafting the original text seem time well spent.

Throughout *Hacking the Human*, I put social engineering into a wider context of information security risk management and countermeasure development. I often referred to ISO 27001 – the international standard that was gaining significant traction at the time – as a suitable framework for this type of activity. I then related the risk assessment phase of social engineering to specific risk methodologies in use by myself and colleagues at the time. This approach was designed to give social engineering a more structured approach, and facilitate business risk communication to senior management.

The extensive application of psychology within *Hacking the Human* was quite new to this emerging field of information security – and something used (and copied) by others since publication.

Another significant theme of *Hacking the Human* was the assertion that training and awareness had only limited value. You will see that in many cases, we simply turn attempts at solving social engineering through training into new vulnerabilities. Hence, a significant part of my role is to help organisations to engineer more systemic protection mechanisms, in order to reduce the reliance on humans within any given systems.

Since *Hacking the Human*, I have turned this systemic protection approach into an academic paper, in collaboration with a university. My more academic approach to research is also reflected in the Part Two of this second book.

After many years in the field, users still come up with some surprising interpretations and modifications to security policies and procedures.

Even last week, I encountered three instances in just one day on site with a client. I was part of a general investigation of user practices for a client with a very well developed information security function, including extensive training and awareness activities.

The first example of somewhat surprising interpretations was a requirement to place confidential information (an output from a particular process) into 'secure storage'. A user at a small satellite site explained the process and showed us the safe in which each day's paperwork was placed. However, I noticed the safe was quite small, so I asked what happened to the same information long-term. The user then explained that at the end of each week, she removed the week's supply of information and placed it in a drawer (unlocked) underneath the safe.

So, as an attacker, you could break into the safe for a week's worth of information, or simply open a draw beneath the safe for what turned out to be a year's worth of data.

In this case, the user had added her own 'sensible' interpretation of the rules, in light of not having sufficient storage capacity in the safe.

The second example of misinterpretation of policy occurred with a telephone process: accepting credit card information prior to processing. The operator being questioned showed me a form that he was to complete with a customer order, and the section at the bottom where he wrote the credit card details.

I asked him what happened to this form, and he responded, "Once I process the payment, I cut off the card details and shred them – because we're not allowed to write card details down." This seemed quite reasonable. I asked him to show me some processed forms, and, as he described, the bottom section of each form had been removed. He clearly was operating according to the instructions.

However, I then noticed that the 'merchant' copy of the card processing receipt had in each case been stapled to the order form. This printed receipt contained the very same card details that the user had removed and shredded. It was a great example of following the rules – but then following up with an action that destroyed the point of the original rule.

These examples show that users are quite adept at modifying rules to fit a given process that they have to complete.
Our third example is a classic 'Post-it note' breach.

A user explained to me that she had to deal with certain credit card refunds, and for security reasons only she (and one other colleague) could do this for their team. Realising that the card details cannot be sent via e-mail (a good rule!), the team had to have a way to transfer the card details to this user for processing.

It turned out that a simple Post-it note served the purpose of data transfer. The user showed me a small pile of these to illustrate how the process worked. Naturally, I asked what happened to these notes, and she replied, "Oh, I shred them at the end of each day, as we are not allowed to write card details down."

Now, the question that springs to mind is how sharing card details on Post-it notes could be aligned with the rule 'not allowed to write card details down'? Clearly, this user did not see a problem with the activity. In effect, she had added a caveat – her rule was clearly, 'not allowed to write card details down, AND KEEP THEM MORE THAN A DAY'.

These examples illustrate, in very simple terms, how users misinterpret and misapply security rules. Their intentions are good, and in no way malicious. They are simply applying corporate policies and procedures in a (to them) sensible way.

This shows that understanding the way the human brain comes to decisions is central to information security. The more you understand the human decision making process, the better you can predict and prevent security breaches.

That is why, in continuing the work of *Hacking the Human*, this new book contains further exploration into human psychology, with new concepts and theories based not only on my social engineering adventures, but also new research and original thinking.

My only regret with *Hacking the Human* was that it was only released under a (quite expensive – sorry) hardback edition. I have to admit to being somewhat socially engineered by the publisher's advance, and didn't read enough of the small print – even I am not immune to these vulnerabilities.

Whilst ECSC did organise a paperback version from the publisher, it was on the condition that it was not made widely available and could be ordered only through my events and on the ECSC website. Therefore, I did insist that *Hacking the Human II* be published as a paperback at reasonable cost from day one

Following the publication of *Hacking the Human*, I have continued to conduct extensive social engineering penetration testing, and remediation consultancy with ECSC. At the same time, my research into human vulnerabilities continues. In addition, my busy presentation schedule has allowed me to continue to update my 'war stories' and theoretical understanding.

I thought it was worth sharing a few words about being a professional social engineer. The adventures within this book will give you a unique insight into how we operate, our methods and techniques, and the results we get. You might think that it all sounds very exciting and glamorous – and you would be right, to a certain degree. When I think of other professions, I count myself quite fortunate. However, it is not quite the dream job you might think.

Firstly, social engineering testing can be difficult – particularly the designing of attacks; the thinking phase of an engagement. Our clients give us a continual stream of new, fresh challenges – and in many instances, these may be things that they believe are not possible to achieve.

I think it is worthwhile to take you through a typical day – the next 24 hours, in fact. As I write this, I am halfway through a five-hour train journey, making my way to a client meeting. Many employees will already be home with their families, starting to relax for the evening. I still have a couple of hours to go, and (even if I wasn't writing this book) would be working throughout the evening.

Tomorrow is the first day with a new client – a major multinational. This is their first foray into social engineering, so they need some guidance and reassurance. We met with them at a conference where I was presenting, and then we did a quick conference call to throw around some ideas. The next stage is for me to spend a day with them. This will accomplish a few different objectives:

1. Learn more about their particular risks, what they see as their most valuable information, and their understanding of the threats they face.

2. An initial exploration of where they think they might be vulnerable to social engineering, and what ideas they have for the tests we might conduct.

3. A chance to discuss how a typical testing engagement would proceed, together with the approach we take to give them the most value.

Now, one of the first things clients want to know is, 'How long will it take?' Clearly, this is an important question. We do have minimum engagement requirements before I get directly involved. This reflects the fact that each of my clients requires a certain amount of my time, just to take into account that I might be exploring ideas for their challenges on an ongoing basis.

We also have ECSC 'SE lite' engagements that bolt onto our technical testing engagements. But I don't directly get involved in these, beyond having designed the outline tests that our penetration testers deploy.

Having a minimum time allocation also reflects that any testing is realistic. Some real-life incidents have taken attackers more than a year to conduct, so a quick two-day test is not going to show much (other than highlight the most obvious weaknesses).

We also don't ideally want clients directing the testing too much. They get better results by giving us some direction, combined with enough scope to be creative. This leads to the discovery of vulnerabilities they wouldn't have considered.

As a starting point, I often explore with clients what someone has to gain from breaching their security, and how much time they might devote to the task. This gives us a benchmark for how much time and effort they should be putting into realistic testing of their particular vulnerabilities.

It is common for testing to be kept relatively secret within a client's operations. Sometimes a senior executive will bring us in without knowledge of the IT team – or even the information security function. However, the most common initial discussions are with the people who do have strategic responsibility for information security – usually together with the appropriate senior sponsor.

Conducting testing in a professional manner is of prime importance, and this needs to be demonstrated from the first meeting. There are some principles that apply to all testing:

1. There should be minimal disruption to operations - we don't want to cost the organisation money (other than our fees). We rarely remove devices, unless we have a specific brief to do so.

2. We should remove the minimum of information. Our job is to demonstrate the weakness. In many instances, we don't have to actually steal information to demonstrate what we can do. So, for example, we often photograph the cover of documents to show we could have removed them, rather than actually stealing them. Where we do remove information, we protect it, and return it as soon as is practicable.

3. It is usually our strong recommendation that nobody is disciplined following our testing. As we are, for first engagements, often conducting our client's first-ever social engineering testing, it is not appropriate to be disciplining people for being 'unlucky' enough to be targeted and tricked.

4. We don't (normally) get involved in any sort of entrapment. By that, I mean that we don't offer financial (or other) inducements to individuals as part of our testing. It is not our job (usually) to uncover people with criminal tendencies.

We also discuss at some length, during the planning phase of an engagement, the potential risks in conducting testing, and build appropriate mitigations into our planning – for example, how we will handle any logins that we obtain. A recent example included us obtaining a number of logins to a system where employees manage their personal salary/share options/ benefits. It was decided that employees would not react well to knowing that a third-party had been employed to try and gain access to this. Therefore, following the testing, a number of messages were communicated to the individuals targeted:

1. The login details were not shared with the company.

2. No login details were used.

3. All passwords obtained were reset the same day.

In developing a social engineering testing practice, it is essential that these professional and ethical principles are adhered to at all times. The nature of the work means that there is no place for individuals with criminal records, or anyone who does not share the highest ethical standards.

You may wonder why a major multinational corporation, with a great deal of very confidential information, were only conducting their first social engineering testing in 2012.

This is a good question, and is indicative of the fact that information security is often confused with IT security, and, more often than not, given to IT personnel to manage. This tends to lead to a very technical focus on both threat identification, and also the selection of suitable countermeasures.

Another factor is that security 'solution' vendors tend to gravitate towards the easiest sale. This tends to be fancy boxes with lots of flashing lights, or impressive-looking software that can be sold on the back of an impressive (if quite unrealistic) sales demonstration.

This often leads to a significant amount of money being wasted in IT security, whilst the human element is neglected.

As you absorb some of my adventures in the following chapters, you might be asking why I am taking the time to produce another book when I have such an interesting and challenging day job.

The answer comprises a number of reasons:

1. Readers of *Hacking the Human* have been asking me, "When do we get book two?"

2. I believe there is still a need, both to share my experiences and also to continue to develop thinking in this important area.

3. The process of writing is a good way to organise one's thoughts, develop concepts, and to enhance the creative element of our consulting approach.

Rather than simply update the first book, I looked at my recent experiences and research, and decided that a new book would be of even more value to the security community.

Therefore, *Hacking the Human II* comes in two parts:

Part One – The Adventures

Each chapter takes you through a social engineering attack, from original client challenge through the analysis and planning phase, to detailed explanations of the techniques deployed and the results obtained.

All of the adventures are based on real social engineering exercises. Real life is so much more interesting than fiction, particularly if you want to understand what is possible with social engineering techniques applied to real organisations.

The only changes that have been made are as follows:

1. I have made sure that nothing is included that could allow anyone to identify our clients – something we take great care with at ECSC. You will understand that our discretion is very important to our clients, particularly in this line of work. There are a couple of instances were I have 'invented' (or changed) a few details, designed to confuse any attempts at client identification. This is where there is a feature of the scenario that might be a little too unique to be left unchecked.

2. In some cases, I have combined the events of more than one similar exercise to give you the best examples, and illustrations, of social engineering tactics and techniques. I didn't want to run through multiple similar exercises just to highlight a few differences.

3. I have also taken some liberties with the individual personalities involved in each adventure. So, if you think I am describing your test exercise, then don't try to match personalities to your colleagues – or yourself. I have mixed up people between the adventures in order to introduce concepts and techniques in a more coherent order. I also wanted to illustrate some key points that might have occurred in two similar exercises, without retelling the whole adventure.

My aim here is to take you through each component of the attack, and, probably most importantly, through the thought processes involved in designing and implementing a successful information security breach.

It may be helpful for you to think about a social engineering attack in two distinct phases:

1. Strategy – the analysis of observed system vulnerabilities, and the design of suitable attack vectors. This requires an overall knowledge of where human weaknesses are likely to emerge within a system, and lead to potential exploits.

2. Tactics – the specific human interactions, using a variety of psychological methods to manipulate individuals. This might be remote through telephone or e-mail, or face-to-face during an on site exercise.

Where an attack involves a particular human interaction, I will also introduce two additional elements:

1. Personality profiling – the categorisation of the individual, whether through remote communication or face-to-face contact. This sort of generalisation is helpful in selecting an appropriate approach.

2. Psychological techniques – the persuasion and tricks deployed to achieve the aims of the social engineering activity. These are closely linked to the profiling of individuals, either based on assumptions or clues from the particular interactions.

The process of personality profiling can be very quick – it might be simply looking at someone: the way they dress, their overall posture; their facial expression. Alternatively, it may be based on analysis of communication – perhaps the language in an e-mail.

Profiling is far from being an exact science, as people can move from one personality trait to another, especially when faced with a challenging situation. However, we are not looking for an 'in-depth' truth when conducting social engineering – we are just identifying aspects of personality that we can exploit, and in turn, improve our chances of success.

In some cases, certain personalities will be assumed, often due to the role of the person being targeted. An executive in an organisation is most definitely not going to have the same personality profile as a security guard. These sorts of assumptions can be useful starting points.

Such generalisations (some might call them prejudice) are justified because they work most of the time, and are helpful to the social engineer. They are what a real attacker deploys, and therefore form a major part of my role in uncovering and fixing vulnerabilities.

Some of the psychological techniques deployed might be quite generic, and could be applied to any individual. However, in many cases techniques will be selected, or modified, in light of the observations regarding personalities.

If you have read *Hacking the Human*, you will recall that I generally use a personality profiling methodology based on work by Marston in

1928, where he characterised people under the headings of Dominance, Influence, Steadiness and Compliance (DISC).

I use a re-working of this system, using the following labels: Driver, Expressive, Analytical, and Amiable.

You know each of these people. Looking at the profiles from *Hacking the Human*, you will be able to identify some typical examples from your own experience:

DRIVER

A driver is primarily a results-driven person, able to make quick decisions (others often think too quickly). They relish a challenge and can be very competitive. They tend to be good problem-solvers and are effective in a crisis. However, their quick decisions can be just as quickly reversed if new information comes to light. They are self-reliant (not needing friends), extremely self-critical, and can therefore appear direct and often forceful. Being risk-takers, they are often adventurous.

EXPRESSIVE

You will find many expressive personalities working within the media and advertising, where their larger than life ego and entertaining side can flourish. They are sociable, generous and often charming. These people tend to have a strong focus on influencing other people, making a good impression to gain recognition and shaping their local environment. In general, these people don't like too much detail and resist control in favour of expressing their own will. Their enthusiasm can also lead to impulsive behaviour.

ANALYTICAL

This person loves to concentrate on key details, thoroughly checking and weighing pros and cons. They like to analyse, adding structure through finding more information. They can take an age to make a decision, as they need to find all the relevant information prior to being able to decide. They consider themselves good decision-makers, and think other people jump to the wrong conclusion without enough thought. However, once a decision is made, they will stick to it, as they must have taken everything into account in getting to that point. They apply the highest standards, with systematic approaches that can border on absolute perfectionism.

AMIABLE

This personality is primarily focused on comfort, creating a stable and harmonious environment around them. They like predictable roles and a loyal group of friends. They tend to like one task at a time, with plenty of appreciation when it is done. They can appear rather passive, predictable and usually very calm.

These four types allow us to position each person in relation to how they are behaving in a given situation. Think of someone at a position within the matrix – they may be on a boundary between two (or more) personalities. They can also move within a range, depending upon their environment and 'mood'.

You might think that some personalities are more susceptible to social engineering than others, and there is some truth to this. Certainly, you could argue that people to the left on our diagram are more likely to use conscious processing, and therefore be somewhat tougher to trick with subconscious communication.

However, each personality has vulnerabilities – they just need a skilful social engineer to exploit them. For example, you might exploit the following weaknesses:

Driver – too quick in making decisions, and not cautious enough, so give them an opportunity to grab!

Expressive – undue focus on how they are perceived by their peers, so make them believe they will look good if they comply!

Analytical – too much attention to detail, without seeing the bigger picture, so tie them up in detail (and become their friend).

Amiable – too quick to comply with instructions, especially if you make compliance the route of least resistance.

We shall be meeting each of these people in our shared adventures throughout Part One, so you will see plenty of examples of how each can be effectively targeted and attacked successfully.

A great example of one of these personalities was the Analytical I was talking with yesterday. I had interrupted him, and he was clearly very busy. I said I would only be a few minutes, so he said he could help. He was in a technical operational role, and I needed some detail on some very specific technical aspects of the client's electronic access control. This wasn't a social engineering exercise – rather, I was helping to design new countermeasures.

Anyway, I had received the information I needed, but along the way, I asked a question that this Analytical couldn't answer – he didn't know how to interrogate the system with the right commands. He was a true technical person - administrating a Linux system at the command line.

I told him that I had enough information. However, he couldn't help himself – he just had to solve this technical puzzle to get the information I had just asked for. Even though he was clearly busy, and I had interrupted him for longer than promised, he insisted on finding the answer. He could not leave some gaps in his understanding.

This focus on obtaining the full information is a feature of the Analytical. It is what makes this individual so well suited to his operational technical security role. He would be a terrible manager, as Analyticals have to make decisions based on less than complete information.

I am aware that personality profiling doesn't necessary get a good press, especially since researchers such as American social psychologist Walter Mischel have found it a challenge to demonstrate a correlation between predictions made using various systems and people's actual actions.

I can only share my experience, particularly where a technique has helped with conducting social engineering.

There are other systems with which to analyse personality, some based on five perceived basic personality traits: extraversion, emotional stability, agreeableness, conscientiousness, and openness to experience. However, I find the quadrant approach works well, as it allows an individual to be mapped at a particular point in their behaviour.

Another aspect to personality profiling is the identification of someone's dominant communication mode – a fundamental of Neuro-linguistic Programming (NLP). This is very powerful, as their communication mode gives you insight into their primary thinking mode.

You will encounter three main types:

Visual – thinks in pictures.

Auditory – uses verbal communication as their primary thought process.

Kinaesthetic – tend to 'feel' their way through life.

You will find the majority of people are primarily visual, with less being auditory and a small minority being kinaesthetic. Spotting them can be often achieved by picking out key words in their communication. Here are some quick examples from *Hacking the Human*:

- '**Shine** a **light** on this issue' – visual

- 'He seems to be **blind** to the problem' – visual

- 'I **hear** what you **say**' – auditory

- '**Sounds** good to me' – auditory

- 'I need to **balance** the issues' - kinaesthetic

- 'Let's get a **firm handle** on this **tough** problem' – kinaesthetic

You will get other clues from people's tone and pace of speech. Visuals tend to talk more quickly, with a higher pitch. Primarily kinaesthetic people talk the slowest, with a deeper tone – be careful they don't hypnotise you! You can often almost hear the singing quality within the speech of an auditory person – it's literally music to your ears.

You will also see/hear/feel (delete as appropriate) throughout Part One that we apply other clues to personality traits. For example, we will deploy the NLP technique of reading eye movements when in face-to-face communication. We will also dispel some of the myths about this, and other, techniques along the way.

Part Two – The New Subconscious

The extensive exploration of popular psychology within *Hacking the Human* has served me well in my adventures. Part one is based on the tools and techniques described in the first book. The mixture of Neuro-linguistic Programming (NLP) and Hypnosis gives you a firm foundation in understanding human vulnerabilities, and in designing a range of social engineering attacks that work. The various examples within *Hacking the Human* illustrated the usefulness of this knowledge, and the adventures within part one of *Hacking the Human II* will give you further insight into human vulnerabilities and associated persuasion techniques.

This knowledge also gives you a framework to design countermeasures – something I focused on extensively in *Hacking the Human*.

However, I was not fully satisfied with this approach to understanding the human mind. Even before the book had gone to press, I had already largely rejected the use of Transactional Analysis (TA) – finding it too simplistic and somewhat observational, rather than a useful tool. I should apologise if you are a TA advocate and convert. However, in the context of my work, I have found it of less use than other frameworks.

My main issue with my previous approach, and something that has continued to bother me, was the concept of the subconscious as a single entity.

The concept of the subconscious as a single entity can be helpful in establishing that our self-perception of our conscious brain isn't completely in control. This alone can be challenged by many people – although I usually counter this argument by reminding them to breathe, because without a subconscious to control this process, they would need to do so themselves (and also remind their heart to beat at the appropriate rate).

Accepting the concept of the subconscious is an important step in explaining behaviour. The next step, outlined in *Hacking the Human*, is to understand to what extent the subconscious is actually in charge of our behaviour. Again, this is challenging for individuals to accept – we like to think we are in control, and our conscious brain will do its best to reinforce this belief. We are all somewhat deluded in this regard. The only significant question here is: to what level are we deluded at each point in time?

Having accepted the relative power of the subconscious, my next step was the analysis of how this could be influenced to direct human behaviour – particularly in our context of information security and social engineering. However, despite extensive success in this area, I was still left somewhat dissatisfied with our understanding of just what constitutes the subconscious, and in particular thinking about it as a single unified entity. This might be how we think about the conscious brain, as we perceive this to be very much a part of our identity – and we don't like to think that we might have multiple personalities (unless a psychiatrist has persuaded you otherwise).

So, where does that leave us with regard to Part Two of this book? It's quite simple: Part Two is an exploration through the subconscious, and the development of a new concept of how it directs our behaviour.

To support this analysis, I have made use of the latest academic research, together with a review back through some interesting historic threads – a departure from *Hacking the Human*, where I concentrated my research on the decidedly non-academic approach to psychology.

As I don't claim to be a full-time psychology academic, you will have to forgive me if there are gaps in my research, or if others have touched upon my ideas previously. What you will find here is my own analysis, and latest thinking, based on the practical application of social engineering techniques.

The adoption of a more academic focus to my research is for two reasons:

1. Academic research has, to a certain extent, 'caught up' with the original concepts implicit within NLP (and also the practice of hypnosis). You can only ignore something for so long if it gets results. Many research findings have 'proved' concepts invented by NLP, and this has then led to other interesting avenues of research.

2. The majority of the NLP/hypnosis community now directs its activities into the (somewhat lucrative) self-help industry. Therefore, I find less and less in the way of original thinking coming out of this area.

Nonetheless, please be assured that I have continued the same, quite accessible, style of presentation of material. It is a style that received praise in *Hacking the Human*, and comes from the fact that I regularly present events to a variety of audiences in many countries, and also regularly have to present the results of my work to senior executives - who like their information in bite-sized chunks (usually pictures), making it easily digestible.

Therefore, the purpose of this journey is to understand behaviour, and the associated human vulnerabilities that can be related to social engineering exploits - and in turn, how we can develop smarter security countermeasures.

In writing *Hacking the Human II*, I deliberately left much of my work on Part Two until after I had captured the bulk of part one. Therefore, you can regard part one as the story so far – my adventures since the publication of *Hacking the Human*. Part Two could be subtitled, *'What Next? Understanding Human Behaviour'*.

I hope that part one entertains you, and makes you think a little (actually, quite a lot). I then trust that Part Two will make you think even more. Alternatively, if you, like me, don't like thinking to be hard, then you can just feel free to absorb the concepts and let your subconscious handle the information. You will understand more about this approach as we go along together.

Looking closely at that last paragraph, you might (as a most intelligent, knowledgeable, and inquisitive individual) have spotted a couple of 'subliminal' aspects to the language. I make no apologies for this. Rather, I trust you will see it as a positive: I practise what I preach.

Hacking the Human and *Hacking the Human II* are full of subliminal 'programming', and influence (you may call it persuasion if you like). Some of this is well thought out and designed on my part, although most of it is automatic – I have now largely integrated this into my communication style at my own subconscious level. However, nothing is hidden – I explain each technique along the way, although not necessarily every time I use it within my own communication.

So please have fun – it makes learning so much more enjoyable and effective. I am confident that you will find the process enlightening.

Feel free to challenge the content – we certainly need more dialogue and critical thinking in this area. I present my own work to further our combined understanding and contribute to the evolution of our shared knowledge.

PART ONE
The Adventures

An Engineer Calls

Introduction

Hackers want access to your systems. By hackers, I mean criminals with malicious intent. Some of you may not like the term hacker used in this context (preferring the term 'cracker'). However, I have chosen to use the term commonly accepted in the media.

An important part of my role is helping organisations, from the most senior executive to the security guard on the front door, understand information security risks and their role in prevention. A critical element of this is the use of simple language and common terms.

Say a hacker wants access to your systems. They will try a number of tactics to accomplish this. Most people think their electronic protection (using systems such as firewalls and intrusion prevention, etc) will prevent unauthorised access. However, most systems have 'back doors' that allow access in an emergency. This might sound dangerous to you, and in some systems these back doors can be accessed from the Internet – so yes, it is very dangerous. However, for more secure systems, these emergency access routes can only be activated if you have direct physical access to the device.

Once given access, an attacker might do a number of things, such as:

1. Remove a device, or part of a device, such as a hard disk.

2. Achieve access in such a way that allows them to either copy data, or set-up access that can be used remotely.

Therefore, a skilled social engineer will want to have on site attacks within their arsenal of weapons.

There is another neat trick that you might come across – an unauthorised 'install'. Most security is focused (for obvious reasons) on preventing theft. So trying to install some new equipment is often viewed with little suspicion – especially if you can create an emergency scenario.

This is one of the reasons why we put our critical IT systems within locked server rooms, or outsource them to 'secure' data centres.

It is fascinating how people often confuse the physical security of data centres with the IT security they provide, which is usually nothing. Data centres are good at providing high-performance connectivity between a hacker and yourself. The physical protection is usually much less of a risk than an electronic attack. If a hosting company, or connectivity provider, does offer electronic protection, it is in my experience normally second rate – it just doesn't fit within their skill set.

A social engineer might also just steal data. Data centres and computer rooms can be a good source of data to steal. Because people perceive them as secure locations, once you have entered the perimeter, you often find confidential data just left for the taking.

Here's a great example of that: I was with a colleague, viewing a potential new office for ECSC. The property in question used to be occupied by a financial institution called a building society (a mutual organisation offering banking type services in the UK). As part of our viewing, we entered what used to be their 'secure' data room – now stripped of all equipment. However, in the corner we found a pile of backup tapes and hard drives. They had clearly been used (as could be seen by their labels), with no indication that they had been wiped.

It was a potential major breach for the organisation involved, and a clear breach of good information security. Being a good information security citizen, I called the organisation's information security manager to alert him to the find.

Anyway, back to our first adventure – this does involve gaining physical entry to a client's 'secure' (and still in use) data centre.

For many years, I have completed a number of client projects in the City of London – not surprising, given the large financial sector based there. Our first mini-adventure came from clients who were concerned with police warnings of fake British Telecom (BT) engineers gaining access to server rooms across the City of London.

For those international readers without knowledge of BT (ex. British Telecom), they are the default provider of connectivity for the majority of the UK. They also always tend to be in charge of the final connectivity wires, even if you buy your communications links from a competing provider. Within the UK, BT are forced to keep elements of their business separate, so in theory, they compete on equal terms on services where there is genuine competition and are not given undue advantage because of their history of monopoly on core infrastructure.

Most companies' external connections terminate in server rooms – so clearly, a BT engineer has potential access to confidential equipment.

Having had a number of 'successful' social engineering exercises with this client previously, they called us with a new question.

The Challenge

"Can you get access to our secure server room in the London head office as a BT engineer?"

On some occasions, we might not accept such a narrow brief – the stipulation of the identity of an attacker might limit our options. It might also be a trick, in that their staff might have just conducted extensive training on this explicit scenario, and might just want our service to prove how effective the training has been – not a realistic test.

We do find on occasion that people don't really want a proper test. Rather, they just want confirmation that they are competent, and to tick a box, so they are able to say they have had a social engineering penetration test. With this existing client, we did know that they had a genuine interest in real results and thorough testing. However, we still did have one question: did they have the budget for us to try long enough and hard enough to succeed?

This statement isn't meant to be flippant or arrogant. We merely wanted to remind the client that any testing exercise is nearly always limited by budget, and it is important to allocate enough time (that equals money) for the test to be realistic.

As is often the case, the main constraint here was time – partly because the client had a fixed budget with other areas that needed testing, and also because we had limited availability to meet the challenge in a short time frame.

I often draw upon the skills of my fellow consultants to assist in social engineering testing. The policy at ECSC is that each consultant needs to be multi-skilled. This keeps us sharp and gives flexibility in deploying resource. Importantly, it also means a consultant can usually help clients, if required, with advice and support outside of the narrow confines of a specific project.

Knowing that the best person to take on the role of an engineer happens to be an engineer, I booked some time in the diary of one of our best.

Another reason for wanting some assistance on this assignment was that I also planned to access the same office myself, in a completely different role at around the same time. I didn't want to meet someone who said, "Weren't you a BT engineer this morning?"

However, at the time of this first exercise, we had no real knowledge of the layout of the office, or the entry procedures. The client was keen to have a near zero-knowledge test, to see what someone could do without any insider advantages.

This is sensible for the first test of an operation, and quite a common client request.

Thinking and Planning

I intend to include this section in each of our adventures. Social engineering could be described as 'the thinking man's security role', given that it brings together so many challenging aspects of system security and human psychology. Therefore, we build 'thinking time' into each social engineering project. We need time to brainstorm ideas and explore avenues of attack. This really can mean the difference between success and failure – after all, you would expect an actual attacker to have spent time in the planning.

Also, I never like to do an attack at too short a notice. My preference is to accept the assignment, meet up with the client to agree the scope, and possible avenues of attack, and then to pause for a few weeks to allow the ideas to flow. This even applies to this, our first, and relatively simple, adventure.

Clearly, dressing up as a BT engineer isn't difficult. You don't even need to know what one looks like at that moment in time, as they likely change their uniforms regularly (following each corporate rebranding exercise), and it is extremely unlikely that anyone on the target site will know the current dress code.

As the client occupied only part of a shared building in central London, access would be by foot, so there was no need to create a fake BT van (although I would consider this equally easy – just a plain white van with some magnetic side boards with the relevant logos on.

We are clearly using the fact that most people will trust a BT engineer, and also trust the corporate branding as an indication of identity.

Working out the internal layout of the office proved to be quite easy, as another tenant had deployed the services of an architect to create a new office layout, and the architect had published this as an online case study. As these types of office often have the same basic layout on each floor, we could at least guess the likely route from lifts to reception – quite important in rehearsing the entry tactics. Also, given the limited time available, any pre-visit on site surveillance wouldn't be possible.

We could also make reasonable assumptions about the location of secure data rooms, although this wouldn't be crucial to the success of the activity.

Attack Strategy

It sounds quite simple – just turn up as a BT engineer, and then say that you have come to fix a problem. You could just ask a friend to do that. Our clients expect us to be a little cleverer than that.

It would be just too easy for someone to respond to the call with, "We haven't reported a fault" – and then insist on making some checks. In my experience, once suspicions are aroused, it can be quite a challenge to manage the situation to a successful conclusion – and I wanted my colleague to be armed with a better scenario than this.

Also, I really don't like it if a test fails at the first hurdle. I have heard stories of this with other testing organisations, and clients take a rather dim view of their capabilities.

Clearly, we needed a little bit more of a realistic pretext, and this is where I came in.

Just think for a moment – why would you allow a BT engineer onto your site? The simple answer is, because you were expecting them. Yes, it really is that simple. If you expected them, they must be genuine. The trick here is to create the scenario where the engineer is expected. Before you jump too far ahead, no, we didn't just cut their communications and turn up before the real engineer had time to attend. As with any professional security test, our activities have to keep business disruption to the absolute minimum, so we can't break things to create a pretext.

My job was to get the client to expect an engineer to be arriving, and then to give him access to the server room. This was to be done with a single phone call to reception.

Another trick here is that once you have convinced one person of your identity, and the reason for your request for access, they then tend to 'introduce' you to others in the organisation. These introductions are powerful, as they imply that some sort of authentication has already occurred. This is a recurring theme in a few of our adventures.

All my associate had to do was dress the part, turn up, and follow directions to gain access.

Execution & Techniques

I have used this little adventure first as it is quite limited in scope. My involvement was a single phone call. Such a limited scope of activity gives me an ideal opportunity to show you the decision-making and thought processes that go into a social engineering attack.

PRETEXT

Social engineering is easy – you just get an idea and try it. If it works, you are a master of human psychology. You only have to look at the numerous e-mail phishing attacks – usually very badly crafted, and obviously fake

– to know that it doesn't take a genius. These attacks work, which is why they continue to be orchestrated.

So if simplistic attacks work, then why go to the trouble to engineer more sophisticated attacks? Well, in some situations – for example, if you only have a single target, you cannot afford to fail. A phishing attack only needs 1% success rate to pay handsome dividends to the attacker.

In this attack, though, my target range was quite limited – probably a single receptionist. Therefore, I might only get one chance at success.

Although I don't like to fail at the first hurdle, in many situations, you do not want a test to be too perfect, as you want to measure the effectiveness of controls. Better to obtain a range of successes and failures. In addition, my role is to understand and uncover a range of social engineering-related human vulnerabilities, and then to help our clients design better countermeasures. Trying the scattergun approach of simplistic tests does not serve this purpose.

However, in this case, I wanted my approach to be a successful first stage of the attack.

Therefore, in our first mini-adventure, my call to the receptionist was not just a case of picking up the phone and saying, "We are BT, and we are coming to fix a problem!" That was just too risky, as it might have been returned with, "We don't have a problem".

As discussed above, social engineering engagements have a sometimes-lengthy thinking phase. This is where my team and I brainstorm attack strategies and work out where they might fail, and how we would react to various challenges.

For this attack, the pretext developed to explain the BT engineering was as follows:

AN EARLY MORNING CALL TO THE RECEPTIONIST

This is important. Early mornings are often staffed by less experienced personnel, and senior managers are often not available to consult if something suspicious happens. In this case, if the message is passed to the IT team, it is likely to be handled by the 24/7 support team who have been on the night shift.

So, the call went as follows:

"Hi, this is John from the BT monitoring centre. I'm not sure if you are aware, but there have been some problems with telephones in the building."

Using your name is friendlier (the person starts to create a belief that they know you). The pretext here is issues with 'telephones in the building' - we don't say 'your' telephones. This gives us the chance to hit on a real problem, but also an opportunity to progress even if the person answering the phone isn't aware.

In making the call, I turned the caller ID function off on my mobile phone, so the receptionist couldn't see any inbound number if her telephone supported this feature.

As it happens, we struck it quite lucky, with the response:

"Yes, we have had tons of problems recently with our phones".

This is the best response we would have hoped for, but couldn't have relied on receiving.

Personality Profile

Yes, as a social engineer you start to profile your target from the first word they speak on the phone – or even before they utter a single word. You can make some assumptions. In this case, the person answering the phone is in an administrative role, so could be an Amiable. However, receptionists sometimes have to deal with conflict, so this is not quite as comfortable a role as a true Amiable would like. Also, this role does involve being 'on show', so a mixture of Amiable and expressive is quite likely.

Then, even with only a single sentence reply, I am beginning my psychological assessment of the receptionist.

The word 'tons' sticks out in the sentence. Why not 'lots of problems'? Tons is a heavy word, implying quite a kinaesthetic mindset. This is also supported by the relatively slow pace of her speech and the relatively low pitch of her voice.

This was quite a surprise, as I might have expected an auditory person to end up in a job involving speaking on the phone. However, it always worth remembering that people do temporary jobs, and often take years to find their ideal role in life. In general, the younger the person, the more likely they are to appear out of place in their role. The person who has been in a role for 10 years or more is much more likely to have found a reasonable fit between the organisational demands and their personality.

If you were to meet her and watch her eye movements, you would be likely to see her glancing down on a regular basis, as she accessed her feelings regularly.

Watching for eye movements is perhaps the most common example of a commonly used NLP technique. It is also likely to be the most misunderstood, and wrongly applied, piece of NLP. In fact, I write this having recently read an example of this model being rejected due to researchers not taking the time to understand it fully.

The mainstream media has just picked up on some research that shows no correlation between eye movements and an ability to detect if someone is telling a lie. They did some controlled tests of the classic NLP model, where different eye movements indicate particular thought processes.

You have probably come across this before. In essence, it states that you can 'read' someone's thought processes by watching their periodic eye movements. For example, people tend to look up when trying to remember something. You can go further depending upon the direction of their eye movement. So, for example, someone looking up to their left is remembering images, whilst the same person looking up to their right is making up images.

Actually, the theory goes further, and says that they 'have to' look up to access those internal memories. This makes you think about the times you might have sat staring (down) at an examination paper, trying to remember what you had revised.

The model, with the accompanying smiley face diagram (see *Hacking the Human I* for more detail), shows a typical mapping of your average person. Academics tested this through the use of controlled experiment. So, if you looked up and to your left, you would be accessing real memories (telling the truth), and if you looked up and to your right, then you would be constructing an answer (lying).

However, the experiment is flawed on two counts:

Firstly, NLP (in its original form, which most people don't bother reading) doesn't say this model is correct. It says that people have their own pattern of eye movements. The model everyone tends to quote might be common, but it certainly doesn't apply to everyone. What about left-handed people – do the results reverse? Sometimes, in my experience, they do.

NLP says that you have to discover someone's pattern by observing them. So, for example, ask them to describe their house, and watch for movement. This gives you 'remembered images'. Then ask them to think what their house would look like painted yellow with bright red dots, and you have 'constructed images'.

Try this, and you will get interesting results. Yes, some people fit the above model, but many do not. In fact, using the example test above, you will actually find some people who say they can't imagine their house painted a funny colour. You can spot this inability to create images with their description of their house, as it also is likely not to include a description of visual aspects. Some people don't (because they can't) think in images.

So testing one model is not a valid test of NLP.

The second reason why the academic research is flawed is that this model of eye movements does not describe the process of lying.

What is a lie? Is it always 'constructing' something?

If you ask me whether I took out £300 from a cash machine today, I can run through the images in my mind of me doing this today (with the associated eye movements) and say yes. However, whilst I was remembering this *activity* today, I actually only took out £200. This 'lie' involved quite a lot of remembered images, with one detail changed – would my eye movements reflect this?

The only (not very reliable) way of detecting a lie is to monitor someone whilst they tell truths and lies (control questions), and then profile their behaviour. You can then spot this similar behaviour with new questions. This is what traditional lie detectors aim to do, through the monitoring of things like breathing, heart rates, and perspiration.

So, back to our target, who was perhaps more Amiable than expressive. I started to move the receptionist further down and right in my personality matrix.

Although this was a very short attack, and wouldn't require any special techniques, my mind immediately started to picture the person talking, their age, dress, education levels; mood on the day.

You might call this guesswork. I might call it expert profiling.

A fairer description would be 'experienced assumptions' that could help progress the attack.

I did meet the receptionist in question during a later attack vector that involved me gaining physical access. Overall, she wasn't a very happy person at work. I still made friends with her instantly (by matching her communication mode). If I were a betting man (which I am mostly certainly not, being well versed in risk calculations, and knowing how much profit our online betting clients make), I would put money on this middle-aged lady spending her leisure time doing some arts and crafts-related activity. Her kinaesthetic thought mode would make this an attractive hobby. Unfortunately, her Amiable personality prevented her from taking the risk of also moving careers into this area.

If you were to suggest this, she would have already worked out a conscious 'excuse' for it, such as,– 'You can't change careers at my age' or 'Changing careers is too risky in the current economic climate'. Yes, these are both excuses, however fitting they may be with an Amiable personalities need for certainty and comfort.

Now, you might be thinking, 'She was just having a bad day' – and that might be true. However, as a social engineer, I am not looking for truth. Rather, I am making assumptions and utilising techniques that tend to work most of the time.

The application of psychology is not going to make you correct 100% of the time. However, it will, as your knowledge and skills improve, move the odds of success in your direction.

Anyway, back to the 'lucky' response of existing telephone issues.

I don't believe in luck. I find it more empowering to regard luck as being the direct result of being prepared with the right knowledge and skills, and then being able to recognise an opportunity. This has been expressed succinctly (by someone else), as:

Preparation + Opportunity = Luck

(I don't claim any credit for this magic formula).

So, with a clear picture in my mind's eye of the person on the other end of the call, I proceeded, tailoring my voice, and language to the other person:

"Well, we have one of our engineers on site to support you in the building at the moment. He tells me that he has identified the problem and is tackling it now. He is coming to each floor to make sure that it is fixed for each tenant.

"He should be with you within the next 30 minutes. Can you let IT know, as he will need access to your connections."

Psychological Techniques

Some kinaesthetic phrases I use, such as 'support you' and 'is tackling it now' help to connect with the receptionist. I also slow down my speech slightly, to match her pace. These are all things that help to make her feel comfortable, and allow her to trust what I am saying.

You might be wondering how I could be doing this sort of assessment, whilst thinking what to say and modifying my communication. It seems like a lot to think about. It is, but your brain is capable of this multi-tasking. You will know that often your mind wanders during a conversation, either to plan what you want to say next, or onto another subject. This is because the brain is capable of much more rapid thought than is needed to support a verbal communication (you have lots of spare processing capacity).

So, you can do some of this consciously and still appear to be completely engaged.

You can also practice this. For example, you can analyse written communication, as this gives you much more time to spot key words. E-mails are great for this, as people tend to use the first words that come into their heads, rather than think too consciously about what they say.

You will also find that the more you analyse people, the more your subconscious starts to take over the process. Eventually, you will be able to do this automatically.

Now, in other situations, I would have entered more of a dialogue – creating a friend and opening opportunities for persuasion and manipulation. However, in this case, I didn't really want the receptionist to have anything other than a normal reaction to the call. Trying to overplay the situation might only lead to suspicions. After all, would someone working for BT dealing with monitoring and faults have time for a chat? Does this fit with their expectations of the format of such a call?

Also, notice that I didn't ask to speak to IT. This was deliberate. I didn't want to create an opportunity for someone knowledgeable to question me on the nature of the problem. Rather, I just wanted the message to be relayed to IT. This could also serve my purpose, as the receptionist might not accurately relay the message. It might turn into "BT are coming on site as they have to do some work", or some other vague variation.

Also, the receptionist might not say where the message has come from – and this helps. Using vague and incomplete language gives the receiving party the opportunity to fill in the missing information with their own assumptions – hence the lack of detail in my call to the receptionist.

It might also help that early in the morning, only a few IT people might be in the building, so the opportunities to check with management might be limited. These finer distinctions and assessment of risks help you stack the odds of success in your favour.

Now, you might be thinking that this sort of process, and analysis, is over the top for a simple call that takes less than a minute. However, it is this sort of depth of thought that leads to the design of effective attacks – something that will be essential as we explore further adventures that present significantly greater challenges.

ON SITE ATTACK

Following my introductory call, my fellow attacker arrived on site suitably dressed as a BT engineer.

Remember, in these situations, we don't try and duplicate the exact uniform of the role we have adopted, as these tend to change regularly. Also, the client is very unlikely to know the detail of the latest outfit. So, a typical engineering-type dress code is fine for this situation. My colleague did have a specially prepared BT engineer's photo ID badge, which he wore prominently.

As it happened, in the course of his research, my colleague found some specific warnings from the City of London police regarding individuals pretending to be BT engineers to gain access to buildings. So we replicated this exact warning on the back of his fake ID badge, together with an 0800 (free phone) number that you could call if you had any concerns. The number was actually one of ours, and routed to our Security Operations Centre (from where we conduct our managed security services), where it could be answered as a 'BT helpline'.

Results & Analysis

Now my chosen colleague is not at his best in face-to-face social engineering – he tends to come across as a bit nervous. I blame this on the effects of copious volumes of sugar, caffeine, and tobacco.

However, in this case, following my call, the receptionist warned the IT department to expect a visit from BT, and my associate was duly met and escorted to the secure server/communications room. In addition, having gained access and the trust of the IT department, he was left unaccompanied. This gave him the opportunity to install a hidden wireless access point, giving us access to the client's network from the nearest coffee shop. It was the same level of access we would have had if we had hacked through their firewall.

We placed a label on the wireless access point saying, 'Do not switch off!' It would take a brave and particularly decisive person to immediately remove this on discovery. If you have read *Hacking the Human*, you will already know that the decisive types will tend to be managing the business, with the IT department being populated by much more analytical types. Also, as this label didn't specify who had made this instruction, it would take anyone discovering the device a while to make sure they weren't doing something really wrong by unplugging it.

(We did, of course, ensure that this wireless access was appropriately secured - so that nobody else could make use of it to gain access. We also had it promptly removed at the end of the exercise.)

I am always interested in where we might have been able to manipulate employees into breaking their own rules (usually expressed in specific policies and procedures). In this case, there was a rule that all visitors had to be escorted at all times – and this particularly applied to 'secure areas' such as the server room.

So, why did the IT engineer leave my colleague alone? On questioning him, it emerged that he had two reasons for this quite simple breach of rules:

1. He didn't regard a BT engineer as a 'visitor'. He understood the requirement for escorting to be related to untrustworthy visitors, and thought he could trust a BT engineer, as they are supposed to have access to their own equipment. This is a classic – 'the rule doesn't apply here' exception.

2. He also expressed an opinion that he, and the IT department, didn't have time to sit and watch every supplier do their work. This is a good example of a 'the rule doesn't make sense here' exception.

These excuses can be thought of on two levels:

Firstly, they can be rational reasons that need to be dealt with through an equally rational organisational response – to review policies and procedures and give appropriate training.

However, there is another explanation. In my experience, individuals can be tricked, manipulated and persuaded to take actions against their conscious better judgment. But when challenged about the incident, they often proceed to apply their own rational explanation as to why they behaved the way they did. It is my observation that these excuses are often an 'after the event' rationalisation of their behaviour, and not a true reflection of the incident in question.

I will be coming back to this theme later. This is partly due to further adventures having some good examples of this concept, but also, in this instance, the face-to-face persuasion was conducted by a colleague, and therefore I am not sure of the exact words he used to engineer the required situation. My best guess is that he somehow reassured the IT employee that leaving him alone was okay in this situation. I do know he has had a good teacher, so I expect he did a fine job.

The concept of a difference between conscious and subconscious decision-making is also something we shall return to, and then explore in great detail in Part Two. However, for now, we shall proceed to another adventure – this time, to extract a large number of passwords without even entering the organisation. This is a low-risk, high return activity for the social engineer.

What Is Your Password?

Introduction

A password is a fundamental of IT security – and until biometrics actually work properly, it is likely to remain a key security countermeasure.

At the time of writing, biometric systems are still largely sold to satisfy people's 'Hollywood' view of security. Regular readers of my online briefings will know about the classic attacks of these systems, such as the jelly baby attack.

For the uninitiated, the jelly baby attack involves the use of jelly baby innards (giant jelly babies work best) to press onto a finger printer biometric reader. The jelly picks up the fingerprint of the last person to use the device. You then remove the jelly, gently blowing on it to dry it out. Placing it back on the reader then gives you the same access as the last person.

I find, for social engineering purposes, biometric systems easy to bypass. I tend not to try anything technical (I prefer to eat the jelly babies).

Because biometrics fail to work properly on such a regular basis, my usual attack vector is simply to use them with the expectation that they will work. I then show suitable frustration at their failure. This invariably leads to the person supervising them to give me access, on the assumption that the system has failed again.

Anyway, returning to the central point of our second adventure, password security continues to be key to how we manage access to a wide range of systems.

As we see an increasing number, and range, of remote access methods to corporate systems, the security of passwords is becoming even more critical. I do not intend to address the benefits of '2-factor' authentication here. This was covered in *Hacking the Human*, including how to use social engineering to defeat a typical 2-factor authentication implementation.

We know that users find passwords difficult. They struggle with what us security professionals call 'strong' passwords – and then, just when they get the hang of their super-duper password, we tell them they have to change it. A lot of information security best practice in this area is actually somewhat wasted, as the people designing the password rules have very little understanding of how passwords are actually compromised, and what constitutes a good preventative measure.

It is not just your average user that finds passwords difficult. IT departments are generally not much better. On a recent engagement, the client IT manager proudly announced that they had recently secured their wireless network with the latest WPA2 encryption technology.

At the time of writing, this is actually regarded as quite good security - and certainly better than the (still in quite common use) WEP encryption that only takes a few seconds to crack.

Unfortunately for the client, my colleague Shaun still managed to hack the wireless within minutes. The issue was not the level of encryption, but the weak password – 'computer' that the client had used. A simple, and easily duplicated, attack revealed this. This is a common thread to much of our penetration testing – systems capable of good security being compromised through poor password usage.

However, one area that organisations are now quite consistently good at is the message to users, 'You must not tell anyone your password'. Users now commonly understand this, and therefore simply asking for a password is becoming less effective as a social engineering technique.

This adventure shows how you can use people's understanding of security and use this against them. A later adventure uses the sample principle, in face-to-face social engineering, to again defeat the users' understanding as to what to do with their password. However, this adventure involves remotely obtaining passwords.

This exercise was, as is often the case, part of a larger exercise. However, this part of the exercise involved targeting users through e-mail to trick them into giving us their login and password details. This is commonly known as a phishing attack.

Phishing attacks are now commonly known to most users. We have all experienced those fake e-mails pretending to be our online bank, or perhaps from a common website, such as eBay. The concept is simple:

1. Send an e-mail that looks familiar in layout.

2. Give the user a reason to click on a link.

3. Direct them to a fake website.

4. Trick them into logging in.

5. Record the logins and passwords for later use (or sale).

If you combine the fact that all users know not to tell anyone their password and also know about phishing attacks, then you would not consider a phishing attack to be a good choice to obtain corporate access credentials. However, this adventure shows you how wrong you might be.

The Challenge

It was a simple brief. "Can you remotely obtain our passwords?" This client had a very well developed information security awareness function, and was confident that everyone knew not to tell anyone their password.

On meeting the client, we agreed that an e-mail approach was a good idea, as this had not been tried before. In addition, this was less time- (and resource) intensive than a telephone approach.

As is often the case where a testing exercise has many components, the adventure as documented here produced results that were then used in other attack vectors as part of a larger testing project. The element of linking different tests to form a larger attack is an interesting element to our social engineering testing, and something we shall illustrate in more depth in later adventures.

Thinking and Planning

We quickly honed in on a phishing exercise as an appropriate e-mail attack vector here. It allows us to target a large group of users very efficiently. You don't need many positive 'hits' to give you access to the network.

Our thinking was based on the knowledge that each user had been trained extensively by the organisation to 'not tell anyone your password'. In addition, we also assumed that every user would be familiar with phishing type attacks targeted at their online banking, or popular (and potentially lucrative) accounts such as Amazon or eBay.

So why choose a phishing attack, given the above? Well, for these reasons:

1. Don't **tell** anyone your password'! We will not be asking anyone to verbally 'tell' us their password, so it will be interesting to see how many people translate 'tell' into 'divulge'.

2. Phishing attacks are well known, but only in specific contexts. Would users translate this knowledge of information security risk into their use of computers at work?

Here, we are applying our knowledge of psychology and decision-making processes to predict likely human-related weaknesses within security. In too many cases, the information security experts will deliver logical messages and training, and then assume an equally logical response from their users. Security professionals often find it difficult to think like an average user. We exploit this weakness.

Attack Strategy

Quite simply, we decided to send users an e-mail with a highly believable pretext for asking them to give us their username and login details. The intention was to trick users into thinking that the e-mail was internally generated.

In classic phishing fashion, the e-mail would explain the reasons for the request, and give them a link to a website that asked for their details. The website would be constructed and hosted by us and match the client's house style.

Copying a website is quite trivial. Each time you access a web page, the code necessary to construct that site is loaded onto your computer. Therefore, creating a copy is simply a case of copying this code. Any images used can just as easily be copied – if your computer can show the image to you, then it has already downloaded a copy.

However, the next challenge is what domain you use. For non-technical readers, the domain is simply the bit of your e-mail address that comes after the @. The same address can be used for hosting a web page, just by adding (usually) 'www.' instead of 'name@'.

You need a domain both with which to receive e-mail, and also to host a website. Notice I didn't say send an e-mail. This is because you can send an e-mail from anywhere and just add whatever sending address you want. This allows you to 'spoof' the sender. However, in our case, we did want to potentially receive replies (mainly to stop the client IT team receiving them), so we did need a fake domain.

We did recognise that you can rely on the fact that most users don't understand how domains work. Critically, they don't understand that the full stop is significant is terms of who owns the site. In addition, where users do understand domains, they still might not spot our fake one.

So, for example, if your company is called XXXProductsInc. you might own the domain www.xxxproducts.com, with an e-mail of ian. mann@xxxproducts.com.

If you are a large organisation, you might create your own sub-domains, such as:

finance.xxxproducts.com, or

securityalerts.xxxproducts.com

Our domain selection relies on the user not knowing that a domain such as:

xxxproducts.securityalertteam.com has nothing to do with xxxproducts, rather it is a subdomain of securityalertteam.com. Only the final portion before the '.com' is the actual registered domain – so the order of parts separated by full stops is crucial.

This gives us the opportunity to register a completely new domain, and then customise it to trick users into thinking that we are part of their organisation.

In addition, we used the assumption that most organisations don't control their use of domains very well, so users often see a number of variations.

This variation in domains can also extend to users being asked to use third-party domains for routine business operations. This is due to increasing outsourcing, where systems are hosted externally, with the provider using their own internet domains. This all combines to create an opportunity to trick the users.

Execution & Techniques

Before we discuss the detail of the e-mail constructed, let's think about our target audience:

Personality Profile

How can you apply personality profiling to a group?

Actually, this isn't quite as silly as it might seem. Firstly, you have cultural tendencies – at a national, local, and organisational level. As I write this, news outlet's are busy discussing a banking scandal, and the merits of mixing the 'cavalier' investment banking culture with the more traditional retail banking approach. I have worked for both sides of the global bank in question, and the differences in culture are very noticeable.

Remember, cultures attract like-minded individuals. I once worked for a government organisation that had a very different culture to the norm. I loved it. However, it was not unusual for 25% of candidates for job vacancies to voluntarily drop out during the selection process, just because of the culture shock they received at interview.

Clearly, you cannot simply draw similar conclusions about each person without seeing their individual characteristics, as we were able to show in the last adventure.

Actually, you can – and I did just that in the last sentence! I decided that you were probably, as are the majority of people, primarily visual in your thinking (and communication). Therefore, I utilised visual communication, as you can 'see':

'**Clearly**, you cannot simply **draw** similar conclusions about each person without **seeing** their individual characteristics – as we were able to **show** in the last adventure.'

This strategy will make the communication more compelling to the majority who are visual. However, it will tend to work against those auditory and kinaesthetic individuals.

So, you will 'see' in the e-mail below that we haven't applied this too much. You will spot a visual word in the opening sentence, but the effect of this single word will not be significant enough to turn off the non-visual reader.

We can't apply our NLP technique of reading eye movements, but there will be plenty of chances to use that in further adventures.

As part of the exercise, we did extract hundreds of individuals' company e-mail addresses from publicly available sources.

Just enter your own domain '@xxxxx.com' into a search engine, and you will see the potentially vast numbers of entries, where the e-mail identities of your employees are freely available. In many cases, you will also find each identified e-mail address is accompanied by additional information about the user – very useful for the social engineer.

This information-gathering phase was to show the client that this information could be quite easily gathered. However, for the actual attack we requested a specific list of users from the client. This was for a number of reasons:

1. It allows the client to contain the test, and know exactly who was targeted. Clearly, this can make debriefing easier.

2. It gave the client an opportunity to test certain groups. They didn't warn us, but they deliberately included all the directors (executive officers) of the company, and also the whole of IT.

Our e-mail simply looked like a new corporate initiative to improve security – very believable, as we all know that information security is increasingly important:

> "As you will be aware, we are always looking to improve our information security. As part of this improvement process, we will shortly be introducing a new system for resetting passwords.
>
> "To use the new system, you must answer a secret security question. The system will protect you from unauthorised password changes.
>
> "In order to set up this system, you must record your question and associated answer, and confirm your security credentials (so we know it really is you setting these up).
>
> "Please visit the following secure web page to complete this process today:
>
> "https://www.XXXX.corporatesecurity.com/SecurityQuestion. html
>
> "The secret security question will be required if you ever forget your password. We recommend choosing a question that is easy for you to remember.
>
> "Thanks from the XXXX Corporate Security Team."

We then directed the users to a page we had hosted, using the corporate style from the main corporate website.

In addition to collecting the login and password details that they gave, we gave them a number of options for their new 'secret' question, such as:

- Date of birth

- Mother's maiden name

- Favourite colour

- Place of birth

This was to ensure that not only did we get their login and password details, but also other personal information – a true test that they had been tricked successfully.

Psychological Techniques

Let's just take another look at that e-mail. At first, reading it appears to be using pretty normal language. You might notice the use of 'you' to personalise the communication (as I do continually throughout my writing). However, there is another level of subconscious (or subliminal) communication going on here.

Let's re-examine the text with some examples highlighted:

"As **you will be aware**, we are always looking to improve our information security. As part of this improvement process, we will shortly be introducing a new system for resetting passwords.

"To use the new system, **you must answer** a secret security question. The system **will protect you** from unauthorised password changes.

"In order to set-up this system, **you must record** your question and associated answer, and **confirm your security credentials** (so we know it really is **you setting these up**).

"Please **visit the following** secure web page to **complete this process today**:"

Now, it is important to stress that this type of communication does not take control of your mind. The reader isn't taken into an instant hypnotic trance, with no choice other than to follow the instructions. This level of subconscious control is actually quite subtle – we are just adding more reasons to comply, influencing you to do what we want.

The aim here is to increase the success rate, so if a normal phishing e-mail gets a 1% hit rate, perhaps we can get 2-3%.

This kind of communication happens all the time. You will know that when you listen to some people, they are captivating communicators, and quite persuasive. This is partly because you agree with them at a logical (conscious) level, but also because they are successfully influencing your emotions through your subconscious.

The technique above gives a series of consistent, and subconsciously compelling, reasons to comply with the instruction.

You will also recognise (yes, those first four words are another instruction – I now do it without thinking) that when you hear some people communicate, you don't really feel like complying with what they are saying. We are very good at making subconscious judgments – some people just make us feel uncomfortable. Politicians are good at this – partly because they lie, but also because they have had really quite ignorant training by so-called psychologists, and political 'experts'.

The best example of this is where a politician smiles because they have been told to. Our recent UK Prime Minister, Gordon Brown, was a great (or terrible!) example of this. He was always a serious, and intelligent, politician (if much too analytical to be the leader), but he didn't naturally smile. However, he had clearly been trained to put on a fake smile – and when he did, the effect was instantly artificial and had an immediate negative impact on the viewer.

You will know, if you have read *Hacking the Human*, that trying to create an effect with artificial body language is very unlikely to succeed. It's much better to just create an internal belief and let your body language naturally follow. So, Mr Brown, stop trying to smile – just be a little happier, and the viewer will intuitively pick this up from you.

However, this incongruent communication can also extend to the written word. Let's look at an example from the phishing e-mail. Rather than say:

"Please **visit the following** secure web page to **complete this process today**",

we might have said something like:

"Please don't forget to do this as soon as possible".

This phrase might seem fine at a logical level. However, the subconscious doesn't understand negatives, so this phrase is actually telling the subconscious to 'forget to do this', which is not very helpful in our persuasion efforts.

The concept of not expressing things in the negative is quite a well-established psychological principle, and something that has led to the rather stupid practice of never being negative, even when trying to tell someone they have done something wrong! This is taking a very 'micro' level communication observation and applying it to a 'macro' level activity. It just tends to confuse the listener, and they are left asking themselves whether they have I just been told off or praised'.

We were supplied with about 1,000 target e-mail addresses for the test. However, we didn't send them all in one batch. This was because we could see that their e-mail was being directed through an external spam filter, and we knew that it could well be set to block a large number of e-mails simultaneously going to all users. Therefore, we sent the e-mails in blocks of 50 with a gap of 15 minutes to the next one – in effect, spreading the attack out over a timeframe of just less than 5 hours.

This had another advantage for the client, as we hoped to be caught. Your role as a professional social engineer is not always to succeed in beating your clients' security. This just shows you are better at security than they are. As my documented adventures tend to be illustrating 'successful' attacks, there is a danger that you get a false impression of our balance between deliberately designing tests to succeed, and others to get caught.

This approach is part of our methodology of creating attack scenarios where the mixture of results allows us to measure your security.

In this case, we knew that not all users would be tricked. Now that users are more aware of the threat, a typically phishing attack might only work in 1% of cases (which still gives the attacker a rather handsome return on their investment in time). But we wanted to see if users would report the attack to either the information security team or the IT service desk (this being the recognised incident reporting route).

In addition, we expected that, once reported, the IT team would issue an attack alert of some kind. Assuming this happened within the five-hour attack window, this would give us the opportunity to measure the effectiveness of the warning, as we should see the hit rate of successful attacks drop significantly after the warning alert.

Results & Analysis

This exercise highlights some of the inherent security weaknesses of Internet and e-mail systems – namely, that internal information and systems are not clearly distinguishable from external systems.

You might argue that we should simply look at the domains being used. However, you need to remember three important factors:

1. Most users do not understand the structure of domain names and addresses.

2. There are now many externally hosted systems that internal users interact with daily.

3. Many of our internal systems are presented with domain names that look external in their construction.

We used this weakness to present users with an external e-mail and associated external web page, and they treat them as internally generated and hosted.

Headline results - 25% of users responded by disclosing their full login details, combined with some other personal information. Compared with a typical phishing attack hit rate of 1% or less, this was quite impressive - and quite surprising, to say the least, for the client.

However, this wasn't the most interesting result of the exercise. About two hours into our sending of e-mails, the IT team issued an urgent alert to the whole company warning them that the attack was happening and not to respond. It took them over an hour from receiving the first report to issuing the alert, because they had to follow an incident plan, and get the response approved by a senior manager.

Interestingly, we had no idea this alert had been sent out, because we saw no discernible difference in our 'hit rate' prior to and following the alert.

It is also worth remembering that some users would have received the attack before the warning, and processed their e-mail in order of receipt. However, our measurement of response rate for those sent after the alert was issued showed no change in response rate.

So why did the attack get such a good response, and the alert such a poor one?

Well, under investigation, it turns out that the IT service desk were so security focused that they sent out a regular stream of security alerts to every user – usually at least three per week. These turned out to be quite technical and, for most users, irrelevant. Users just don't need to know the technical details of a fancy new virus – and don't even need to know it exists if they can't do something to prevent it.

What the IT team had effectively done was to condition their users to ignore alerts, as 99% of them were of no use to the users.

There were other elements to the results that make interesting reading.

The information security manager (who jointly commissioned the test with the CEO) received an e-mail from an information security co-ordinator at a remote site. This person was the manager's 'eyes and ears' on the ground – responsible for compliance with policies and procedures, together with guiding and supporting the users on his site. So initially the manager was pleased that the co-ordinator had spotted the attack and was contacting him to report it.

Unfortunately, the communication was not to report the attack. Rather, the e-mail simply said:

"I saw the security notification this morning, so I have made sure everyone here has completed it today. For anyone who isn't here today, I will ensure they complete it on their return.

Regards

XXXXX"

Clearly, the security co-ordinator had been fooled by the relatively simple phishing e-mail. And yes, as you might have guessed, he had also ignored the IT department's security alert regarding the attack.

We also obtained some interesting results from individuals. In one case, someone replied directly back to the e-mail, pointing out that he used three different main logins because of his technical role. (Yes, one of them was a domain administrator login).

We simply replied: "That's fine, just complete the process three times".

We then watched as his details came flooding in. A domain administrator login is always a nice result.

To top off the exercise, we even received e-mails from people who hadn't been targeted. Well-meaning colleagues had forwarded them the attack e-mail.

We do like it when a plan comes together. You should consider how well this attack would work for your organisation.

May I Ask You A Few Questions?

Introduction

For this adventure, we are back to on-site testing – my particular favourite social engineering activity. I find the combination of planning the 'break in', combined with the challenge, and diversity, of interacting with a range of individuals 'face-to-face' particularly satisfying.

In the first mini-adventure, I described my role in designing and facilitating the attack, with a colleague doing the interesting bit. In this, case my role was to carry out the whole attack. I was working alone for this aspect of the client engagement. We usually like to work in teams (even if just in pairs), as it gives more opportunity to discuss tactics and come up with new attack vectors. However, on occasions, we do work alone.

In the last chapter, we explored the limitations that users place on their interpretation of 'do not tell anyone your password'. This is a weakness we shall exploit again here, but in a completely different way.

An interesting aspect of this engagement was actually what had happened before we were engaged. The client in question had commissioned a previous test from another provider. However, they had some suspicions that the individuals involved might not be as expert as they professed to be. Therefore, they had insisted on a 'payment on results' arrangement.

Now, the fact that a supplier agreed to such terms should have raised further suspicions – but the client took the view that they had nothing to lose. And sure enough, they really had nothing to lose (including any information), as the testers failed to gain any access or extract any information. I still consider this to be a waste of time for the client, so don't recommend this approach when you buy social engineering testing services.

Having had this negative experience, they gave us a call – and suggested a similar arrangement. We refused. Rather, we gave them the benefit of our some of our experiences, and explained the nature of our engagement process. This gave them enough confidence to commission our services on a more usual business arrangement. Whether they were more convinced by my measured, consultancy approach, or by our sales people assuring them that we had never failed, I am not sure.

This adventure is also a good example of a nicely formulated client brief. My preferred client engagement is a combination of a specific target (sometimes called 'capture the flag') and a wider objective of 'just see what you can find'.

Both of these types of objectives have their benefits:

- Capture the flag - this can give you a dramatic result that can be useful in engaging senior managers and focusing people's attention. The target may be very specific, and this can create a nice challenge for me as a social engineer. Where there is a team of us involved, we might have a little friendly competition to see who can get the prize first. The negative aspect of this approach is that the focus can be too narrow to have wider organisational benefits – you tend to find the most obvious route of attack and exploit it.

- What can you find? Here the main benefit is that a wider range of vulnerabilities can be uncovered. This often includes areas that the client may not have contemplated. It also gives the opportunity to measure different results across varying user groups. In some instances, not only have we discovered vulnerabilities that hadn't been considered, we've also uncovered critical information that the information security function didn't recognise as exploitable.

The Challenge

"Gain access to the headquarters, and get hold of our client database information – and see what else you can do."

A nice, simple brief, with a combination of specific target and general interest in what could be achieved.

In this case, the client was in the financial sector, and managed a large volume of client funds. Therefore, they had an extensive database of clients. This was perceived as their most prized asset. Our task was not to try and access individual funds, but rather to extract their client information.

Thinking and Planning

We had very little information about the office, the teams present or specific vulnerabilities. However, as is often the case, I did have an opportunity to visit the client to discuss the engagement and float some ideas for approaches.

It is my practice when making a pre-engagement visit to arrive 30 minutes early. This gives me a good opportunity to observe the operation of reception.

Currently on my desk, I have two pages of notes from doing such a visit to another client. These notes include:

1. A drawing of the external office environment, with car and pedestrian access routes and location of security personnel.

2. A diagram of reception, with access routes and description of the observed process for staff, visitors, and contractors.

3. Details of how the swipe entry and visitor entry work, both through reception and into the main work area.

4. Sketches of four different staff and visitor badge combinations (and lanyards), together with how each type of person interacted with reception and gained access (or exit).

5. Observations on to the activities of the receptionist – how observant she was, whether she also answered the phone whilst operating reception, and how much attention staff received in addition to visitors.

6. Conclusions about the 'quality' of the security guards, and their level of attention.

7. Outline observations of the normal office dress code.

I would then use these, usually in combination with some site surveillance at specific times of the day, to develop a range of strategies for breaching the reception entry controls.

So, back to our adventure. I was equipped with my usual observations from a previous visit. A receptionist and two security guards manned the reception. There was also a barrier entry car park with rear door-only swipe access.

As I knew very little about the internal workings of the organisation, I did need a pretext, or identity, that would help me extract information, and give me the flexibility to interact with a number of people.

I decided to be an auditor from the large financial auditors that audited this organisation each year. The identity of these auditors is quite easy to find out, as they co-sign the annual accounts. This identity gave me a number of advantages:

1. Auditors ask for information. In fact, for most employees that is all they think an auditor does.

2. How do you best deal with an auditor? Quite simply, you give them the information they ask for and they leave you alone. This means that organisations effectively train their employees to give up any information an 'auditor' asks for.

In addition, as a new auditor, I had a convenient reason for not really knowing much about the organisation. So I decided to be an auditor on my first day.

I prepared some fake business cards – although these were not copied directly from a real auditor from the chosen 'big four' audit company. This is not necessary, as my targets are very unlikely to have anything to compare my fake with.

Attack Strategy

Despite my new identity, I decided that I needed more information regarding the internal layout of the office, so I elected to do a pre-break in prior to the main attack. As I intended to arrive in the area the evening before, I thought this would be a good opportunity.

Of course, I did ensure that the official client communicated attack start and end times did include the evening before. I never do anything outside of the agreed testing timeframe.

So, how to break in the night before? I made some assumptions:

1. A professional services organisation is likely to have people working late. (Plenty of lights on in the office confirmed this assumption).

2. After 18:00, it is likely that a security guard will be on reception, rather than the receptionist.

3. In a reasonably large organisation, the security guard will not recognise everyone.

The layout of reception was as follows:

1. A revolving door, leading straight to the receptionist/security guard desk.

2. A swipe barrier entry gate to one side, in clear view of the reception.

Therefore, I needed to have a reason for the security guard to give me access. So I needed an automated break-in tool – otherwise known as a cup of coffee.

I approached the office in just a shirt and tie (no jacket), and carrying only a cup of coffee (no bag). Now the only time people come into an office like this (especially in winter) is if they have just 'popped out'.

I was also in the middle of a telephone conversation.

Actually, it was more of a stern dressing down that I was giving (a fictitious) person.

The security guard saw me approaching, coffee in one had and phone in the other, shouting my displeasure at someone on the phone.

Personality Profile

My strategy was pretty much decided at this point. I had not had a chance to observe this security guard in action. However, I had made some generalisations regarding his likely personality profile, which was decidedly Amiable.

We did make eye contact. I intensified my look slightly, into a bit of a stare. His first reaction was to look down, which meant he was accessing his feelings. This is quite a subordinate reaction. If you have a dog, you should try this. I am not trying to put this person down by comparing him to a dog. However, you can spot similarities in our automatic responses to a perceived threat through the wider study of other animals.

Anyway, my quick, intense stare at the security guard produced the reaction I wanted – a clear signal of subordination. He was not really suited to the role.

Remember, security guarding in a UK office environment, is particularly boring – and very poorly paid. This tends to lead to individuals being in these roles who are the least suitable from a personality perspective, and they rarely pose any sort of serious challenge for a social engineer.

Now, to the magic words that would gain me entry! Actually, I said nothing. Rather, I just indicted my desire to be let in. I would have explained that I had left my badge at my desk if challenged. But the combination of my dress, confident attitude (and a mean stare), and my overall stern demeanour was enough for the guard to press the magic button on the reception desk and let me in.

Psychological Techniques

Beginners in social engineering tend to try too hard, and often complicate their social engineering – convinced that they have to deploy every trick in the book with every human interaction.

Remember, sometimes less is more. Trying too hard can raise suspicions, even at the subconscious level for your target.

You should select your role, and the pretext for your behaviour, and act in an understated way wherever possible.

From the perspective of the security guard, the indications were that I was just returning. Did he really want to have my obvious displeasure at the person on the telephone directed at him if he challenged me? This would have meant interrupting my call.

Now, having been let in, I proceeded to make my way through the office and get a feel for the layout. Immediately, it became obvious that this wasn't going to be a 'normal' test – the client had evidently just completed an extensive information security awareness programme based on social engineering. This was clear from the fact that every floor had a number of posters describing the need for the 'human firewall' - with a design that looked like it had been taken from the cover of *Hacking the Human*.

This didn't worry me unduly, as I had a strategy in mind for the next day, and I thought that, with some modifications to my intended approach, the recent awareness exercise might even be used to my advantage. Turning protection attempts into vulnerabilities is one of the most satisfying aspects of successful social engineering.

The pre-attack break-in also paid dividends, as each floor contained a diagram of the office layout and location of specific teams. I simply photographed these with my mobile phone and had a walk around to absorb the environment. This sort of activity is really nothing more than acclimatisation. With enough experience, you get a feel for an organisation by observing the office environment, and you start to understand the likely culture you will encounter as you begin to interact directly with the personnel. My priority was simply to observe the environment and get a sense of what I was likely to encounter the next day.

I did not intend, at this stage, to directly engage in human interaction, or take opportunities to remove information.

Having felt suitably acquainted with the office, I left – this time through the rear entrance. This avoided the swipe entry and only required a push button to exit. It also allowed me to see more closely my intended first entry route in the morning.

Execution & Techniques

Now to the main attack day.

My first job was to gain entry again, using a different route and technique. This is important, as my job is not just to break in – it is to assess security and highlight vulnerabilities. Therefore, I had another two entry routes planned for execution that morning.

The rear entrance wasn't much more than a tailgate entry. I had noticed a cycle rack area to the rear, and assumed that between 8:30 and 9 a.m., a number of cyclists would enter through this route. It is a feature of fancy reception access control systems that, due to their cost, they are rarely implemented at each point of entry.

It turned out that people parking their cars in the small car park also used this back door, so I could walk through this route and gain entry. I used a fake employee badge for this, created from my notes taken on the pre-sales visit. It wasn't even an actual swipe badge – just a printed paper copy.

This entry did allow me to 'deposit' my bag in the office (in a suitable location) for later collection. I had some resources that I wanted to use later in the day, but didn't want a bag for my next entry test – back through reception.

So, having left the bag, I again left through the back door, so I could return to the front reception. I wanted to try a number of entry techniques to give the client some comparative metrics.

There is a risk that an unattended bag could cause an alert. This is unlikely in an office like this, especially as I am good at placing them so that they don't attract attention. However, just in case,   I do leave a note inside as to what the purpose of this collection of items is. Thinking of potential risks to your client is an important aspect of any security testing engagement.

This time, I wanted a variation on entry, so I became a visitor.

My visitor badge was simply created using the photographed images I had taken of my badge on the pre-visit.

For this attack, I wanted to approach reception mid-morning, when the receptionist and two security guards were present. This would be a visitor returning back to the office.

I approach the receptionist directly (with a paper file), and said:

"Sorry, I just had to get something from my car – can you let me back in? I know where I'm going." My visitor badge was clearly visible.

I made some assumptions here:

1. The number of visitors is probably quite large, so the receptionist wouldn't remember me.

2. Although there might be a rule that visitors need to be escorted, she wouldn't want to annoy someone (who might be quite senior) by insisting that they come back down to reception to collect me again.

Personality Profile

Quite a typical receptionist. A little too much make-up, giving away her Expressive personality leanings.

She clearly wanted to be found attractive by the opposite sex, and believed she was. Therefore, the best strategy was to fulfil her expectations and treat her as very attractive.

In other situations, I would have developed a conversation. However, I didn't want to give her any chance to question me as to my contact within the organisation.

In this case, my chosen strategy was simply a smile to confirm a level of attraction.

She proceeded to open the swipe entry gate and let me in.

Now, I really like swipe barrier systems. Firstly, they are easy to bypass. But, more importantly, they give employees on the inside a false sense of security. They believe they are within a secure perimeter, and are therefore naturally trusting of someone already on the inside. I would use this to my advantage.

Having gained access three times using different routes and techniques, I could now focus on the inside element – obtaining access to the client database of information.

As you know, the previous 'social engineers' had failed to obtain any client information. So I decided I would aim to obtain all of the client information. I was determined to establish at the first opportunity that the client had indeed chosen the right people for their testing.

Also, having managed to successfully 'break in' using a few different techniques, I was now feeling quite relaxed and up for a challenge. The question was, therefore, how to gain access to the entire database.

I usually find it best to target the wrong person.

Yes you did read that correctly – let me demonstrate the technique:

As I now knew, from my previous evening's surveillance activity, the internal layout of the office, I had identified the location of the Database Administration Team. So I proceeded to the floor above and approached a member of the IT Service Desk. These people (believe it or not!) are actually trained to be helpful – they are also quite often junior within the organisation.

I selected my target, principally for some physical characteristics that told me he was quite easily led.

Personality Profile

Yes, that was his rather large size. In today's environment of sophisticated (social engineering) marketing techniques by the food industry (and other addiction-based products), it takes a relatively strong control of the subconscious to maintain a healthy weight.

For most developed countries, tobacco has become less attractive as the legal drug of choice to push onto the (subconsciously weak) masses. It has been replaced by sugar, caffeine and alcohol.

If you want to demonstrate mastery of your own subconscious, and sharpen your physical and mental body, my advice is to replace these three damaging substances with healthy and energising body fuel, combined with enjoying exercise.

Anyway, back to my choice of target.

If I had to place him in the personality profile matrix, he would be at the bottom, between Amiable and analytical. In a technical role, he would be a good candidate for Analytical, but his weight and facial expression on greeting me said Amiable.

More on this in Part Two, so without being offended, if you consider yourself overweight, let's just say weight was a factor in my choice.

Actually, perhaps you should be offended? If you have something about yourself that you really want to change, then it doesn't help you at all if people are nice about it. You need to build a deep level of dissatisfaction so that your subconscious gets clear messages to help you 'change your mind'.

With so much social engineering experience, I now trust my judgment – both conscious and subconscious. I will often target a person because of the general 'feel' I get from them, and this young man gave me a feeling that he was just waiting to comply with my requests.

"Good morning, I wonder if you can help me?"

Quite straightforward, courteous and non-threatening. However, it also contained the command 'you can help me'.

"I'm doing some audit work for XXXX. This is my first day, and I am not sure whom I should be speaking to. However, I need to do some transaction queries from the client database. Are you the best person to help me?"

Dropping in that it was my first day was deliberate – even though I was not in my first day as an employee, the same sympathy applies to anyone new (even an auditor!) I am sure you can remember what it feels like on your first day in a new job – and therefore, you naturally feel some empathy and a desire to help someone else in this situation. Here I am assuming you are in a professional culture, and not in the sort of job that takes delight in tricking new employees at every opportunity.

Anyway, back to our rather portly helpdesk operator. His response was somewhat helpful:

"You need to speak to the database team. They're on the second floor. Would you like me to take you down?" Jackpot!

Two minutes later:

"Hello Fred, this is Ian. He is doing an audit for XXXX, and needs to speak to you."

I hope you can now see why you should, on many occasions, target the wrong person. If handled correctly, it can lead to the perfect introduction.

Fred had no idea that my new service desk friend had only just met me. If a colleague introduces someone to you, your natural assumption is that they do know this person.

Now it happens that Fred was the head of the database administration team, and was only too pleased to help. He sat me down, and fired up the relevant screen to start interrogating the database, in all its glory.

"What exactly do you need, Ian?"

Personality Profile

Wow, such powerful force used on the word 'exactly' – it was almost aggressive. We were moving well up from the expected Analytical into the realm of Driver here, which was not completely unexpected, from the head of a team.

His sharp looks and trim dress backed up the Driver personality. His posture said he was in control and ready for action. My arrival was the next challenge, to be dealt with quickly and efficiently.

His visual focus was confirmed through our conversation, as he always looked up, in quite an exaggerated way, when I asked a question. Clearly, his mind worked in pictures.

Psychological Techniques

Drivers like to lead, so letting them take charge and being a little subordinate can work wonders. This can also be complemented with matching his communication and thinking style, so don't be too subordinate – just a slightly less of a driver than him.

Matching the personality of your target can be a powerful way to establish rapport. I am not talking about the rather silly, and very easy to detect, matching of body language. Matching their thought processes and communication style is so much more powerful. Don't think about body language – let it take care of itself. You will actually find that they follow you, and match your body language (without consciously realising that they are doing it).

"Well, to be honest, I'm not really sure. This is my first day here, and I've been given some rather vague instructions. Basically, I've been told to find out about transactions from the last month.

"I think a colleague is going to use this as a starting point to select clients' transactions to look at more closely. But I don't really know much more than that. What do you suggest?"

Fred proceeded to do a query and select the full information for each client, along with a summary of their transactions for the last month. It came to about 40 pages of data.

"Does this look okay to start with?"

"Yes, that looks fine to me. I presume I can pop back to see you if I need anything else?"

"Sure. Do you want this on a memory stick?"

"I had better not, I don't think we're supposed to use these now for security reasons. Can you print it out for me?"

Fred proceeded to print the 40+ pages. I thanked him and left.

My next port of call was the office of the Information Security Manager. I simply walked in and placed the pages of client information on his desk.

He looked at me and slowly shook his head.

"I knew this was coming when I saw you sitting next to Fred a few minutes ago".

The purpose of my immediate presentation of the information to the manager was not just to show off. Rather, it was part of the professional approach to testing that means we never remove information from a client site unless absolutely necessary for the testing.

Now, I had just broken in through a number of routes, and then gone straight to the heart of the most valuable information and obtained it all – and it wasn't even time for lunch yet! So what next?

Actually, this is pretty much what the client asked, as he knew that the whole day had been allocated for this test.

"I would rather like to get as many passwords as I can. Is that okay?" was my response.

You see, having seen all the posters about the 'human firewall', and others reminding people not to tell anyone their password, I had a cunning plan.

Having left the office the previous evening, after my surveillance operation, I had been straight on the phone to a colleague from ECSC:

"Can you write me a quick application?"

"Sure, when do you need it for?"

"First thing tomorrow morning, please."

My team is very understanding of my evening calls for assistance and advice – and always very helpful.

So, armed with my new 'killer app' on my laptop, I proceeded to my first victim (sorry, that should be testing subject).

"May I ask you a few questions?"

I pulled up a chair and opened my leather folder. I made a point of not introducing myself. Instead, I pointed my pen at the blank piece of paper in my folder. To the side, my business card was visible in a small window. The subject saw this, recognised the logo, and with my question, knew this was yet another audit.

Remember, my challenge here was that the surveillance showed evidence of extensive awareness activities, so I decided to use this to my advantage.

"I understand that you have recently had training in information security?"

"Yes, that's right."

"Good. I'm here just to ask you a couple of questions about security, as we've been asked to audit the effectiveness of the training.

"Don't worry, you can't fail the audit. We aren't using anyone's names in our report. This is more about whether the training has been effective, and to identify gaps or potential improvements for future training."

The above is an example of my opening statements. However, they do vary according to the individual I am faced with. As I worked my way through the office, I sampled 20 different people in different departments. This was enough to be representative and give the resulting metrics some validity.

Of course, I didn't just jump in and ask for people's passwords – that would be too obvious. Remember, I had my 'killer app' card still to play.

I started by asking people to explain their role, as this was my first day auditing this organisation, and I didn't really understand the operation. Giving people something familiar to talk about is a good way of getting them more relaxed.

If you have studied *Hacking the Human*, you will know that I don't go along with the simplistic (and easily detected) approach to body language as a way of developing rapport. Rather, I just develop rapport, and then let my body language (and my target's) develop naturally. The best way to do this is just to find things to really like about the person. Your subconscious will then automatically communicate this to them through your body language. Their subconscious will interpret this as genuine, rather than making them feel uncomfortable, in the way that artificially crafted body language tricks have a tendency to.

By asking people about the security training they had received, it also enabled me to explore topics such as the most confidential information to which they had access. As part of this discussion, I could say:

"Can you show me how you access these files, as I will need to check with IT that the access controls are set correctly on these folders?"

This enabled me to collect examples of confidential information that could be accessed once I have obtained their login and password.

So, having conducted a nice friendly discussion, with about 7 or 8 questions, they were very relaxed, and could see that I was a nice chap (not like those other horrible auditors that they might have encountered). Then came the critical stage:

"As part of the audit, I have been asked to try and trick you into giving me your password."

Yes, I tell them what I am about to do. Sounds crazy, but there is a logic to my strategy:

"However, I think this is unfair. I'm sure you know that you shouldn't tell anyone your password?"

They confirmed this.

"So, if it's alright with you, I'm going to say that I tried to trick you and you refused to tell me your password. Is that okay with you?"

At this point, they thought I was the nicest auditor in the world. Actually, I was just the most devious:

"However, I do have to do an analysis of a group of passwords, to see if they are strong enough. But don't worry, you don't have to tell me your password. I have a secure way to analyse passwords."

At this point, I opened my laptop and revealed the XXXX Password Analyser – newly written by my colleague the night before.

This was a simple dialogue screen with the name of the auditing company and the title 'Password Analyser'.

"This takes your password and immediately encrypts it, so I can't read it. Then at the end of the day, it gives me statistics as to how many passwords are suitably strong. Our report just includes these figures and cannot be used to identify individual users."

I then pass them my laptop, and make a point of looking away. (What a nice auditor!)

The little app requests their network domain login, and then their password. It then presents a dialogue box saying: 'Password Encrypted'.

Of course, the reality is that the application has just stored the login and password details to a plain-text (unencrypted) file on my hard disk.

In the course of my mini-audit, I did receive a challenge from a manager/supervisor. They spotted me taking a seat next to one of their team. This person was primarily charged with providing telephone support to clients. They tended to be quite closely monitored, often with records of their allocation of time through the day. So I wasn't too surprised to be challenged.

The manager was not happy. I think this was partly due to the fact that I had picked someone who looked quite apprehensive (it turned out that he had only been on the job two days).

The manager objected to an audit without warning, and also clearly felt quite threatened that I had picked on her newest recruit.

She insisted on knowing whom I was working for, and wanted to speak to them before letting me carry on.

Personality Profile

Clearly quite a Driver, she wasn't really dressing to impress, so wasn't leaning towards Expressive. Her focused expression reflected some Analytical tendencies.

You could just see her conscious brain taking control, looking for logic, and waiting to make decisions based on my answer. Not an easily led personality.

Rather than try and trick her, I decided I had better show her my letter of authority for the test:

Dear Employee,

THIS IS A SECURITY TEST

If you have been shown this letter, then I must personally congratulate you on being vigilant and aware. We need more people with your attention to detail to protect our information assets, and keep our people secure.

We have employed XXXXX to test our security. You will understand that to make this a true test, we could not warn you. The person showing you this letter will make a note of your details, and your successful detection of the test will be reported to the management team in their final report.

I ask you to keep the details of this test to yourself, as even your line manager will not be aware of this exercise. Your support in our efforts to enhance our security is greatly appreciated.

Yours faithfully,

Chief Information Officer

The letter was of course presented on a mock up of the client's headed paper, which was quite easy to do.

Yes, this letter was part of the test, to see if the manager would allow me to continue without actually checking with anyone in management.

I took her to one side and showed her the letter, then smiled as she glanced up from reading it.

"Wow, this is exciting, isn't it?" she declared, relaxing her look and starting to enjoy the situation in which she found herself.

"I have heard about this sort of thing, but I didn't think we did it, too."

By this point, she was clearly both relieved that it wasn't directly an audit of her team, and that she had 'passed' the test. She added:

"Do you actually get paid to do this? That is amazing! When can I tell people about it?" she asked.

"The end of the week should be fine", I replied.

She explained that my original target was very new, and therefore hadn't actually been through the full security induction yet. I said that was fine, in fact it was better if I tested a wide range of people. I added that my report wouldn't highlight individuals or specific teams.

She was very pleased with this (and still quite excited that someone could make a living out of doing this sort of work).

I do, of course, have a genuine letter of authority on my person for each on-site social engineering test. This is similar to the fake one above, but actually issued by the client. The main differences are the inclusion of:

1. The exact start and end dates and times of the testing.

2. The details of the ECSC personnel carrying out the test, including the fact that we will each be carrying photo identification.

3. A list (usually quite short) of everyone within the client organisation that knows about the test.

4. An instruction to contact one of the named people to confirm the test is genuine, before letting us proceed. (And a reminder to use the internal directory for contact numbers, not just a number supplied by us!)

Another manager challenged whom I was working for, but not in a way that caused me too much trouble:

"Who are you here working with?" he said. This sort of challenge can be accompanied with a range of other non-verbal signals. These give you a clue as to how suspicious the person is. In this case, it was more about asserting their perceived authority.

Personality Profile

The worst kind of manager – you might have met one in your organisation. The extreme Expressive (although convinced they are a Driver, if they have been exposed to personality profiling). Frustrated that they don't progress higher up the organisation, they blame everyone else, when they should be examining themselves.

Psychological Techniques

The great thing about Expressives is that they usually believe that they are right. Therefore, they have a wonderful tendency to answer their own questions.

In many cases, they just like to impose some authority, and need to believe that they have demonstrated some superiority over other people.

"I am not sure, this is my first day", I responded.

"Is it the audit team on the first floor", he suggested.

"Yes, that's right, but I don't know who our main contact is", I replied.

"That's okay, it is just that I have to check these things." Then he just let me carry on.

It is quite interesting how many challenges include the challenger giving you the right answer if you give them the opportunity to do so. In many cases, just saying you don't know who is your contact is enough for them to give you a suggested answer.

Results & Analysis

The variety of physical entry tests worked well, involving a range of personnel, including security guards and receptionists.

My techniques assumed an element of tailgating (for the rear exit), but also tricking my way through swipe barrier systems. I am relying here on the fact that.

1. Receptionists and security guards do allow people through barrier systems under certain 'acceptable' circumstances. I just had to find out what these were.

2. If you look, and act, as if you have a genuine reason for access, then most people comply with your request. In general, they don't believe they are there to protect against smart-looking people in professional attire.

Accessing the client database showed another weakness of barrier access systems: they make people on the inside too trusting of other people. They develop the belief that they are within a secured area.

This is combined with the organisational conditioning that the best way to get rid of an auditor is to give them everything they ask for.

The results of the password audit?

"You must think I am stupid", said one target.

"Actually, far from it", I replied. "In fact, you are clearly of superior intellect, as I have just tried the same technique on 19 of your colleagues, and you are the first to refuse to comply".

Did she posses superior social engineering defences? Perhaps. Or perhaps I was just getting a little bit bored (or complacent), and didn't perform as well. Let's give her the benefit of the doubt.

I even considered the possibility that I wanted someone to challenge me, and therefore gave her signals accordingly. After all, I do always say that a successful social engineering testing programme produces a range of results, so you can obtain some meaningful measurement and metrics of your actual security level.

Anyway, 19 out of 20 is a 95% 'success' rate, so I can't complain.

Of course, being on the inside, I could have used any of these login/ password details to access the network and steal information. In addition, as my 'audit' questions had revealed the most confidential information people had access to, I also knew where to look.

However, on this occasion, actually accessing the information would have being a little bit beyond my brief. This might be tempting. However, is likely to lead to you leaving doubts within the client as to the risks of other exercises being extended into unauthorised areas. Instead, I proceeded to the office of the Information Security Manager to let him know the names of everyone who needed to be debriefed (and have their passwords reset – essential as I now knew them and don't like to leave with live passwords).

I made a point of recommending that the lady who passed the password test receive a prize of some sort. I understand she received a bottle of something bubbly – well deserved.

Oh, and finally: The client did thank me personally for *not* agreeing to payment by results. This is after they saw the volume of information that I had obtained, and worked out the potential cost of this original payment request.

Hacking The Cloud

Introduction

Isn't the 'cloud' wonderful? It's a triumph of marketing; a fantastic example of turning something (third-party hosted systems) with serious concerns about security and rebranding it as something new, exciting, and 'the future'.

I love the work of professional marketers – in a few cases, they are masters of social engineering. Recently I watched an advert on television for what used to be – and, given that its ingredients haven't changed, must still be – a rather cheap and nasty cider. It explained how a major benefit of this cider was that it contained so many types of apple. Now anyone who knows anything about cider knows that the best cider will contain a single apple variety from a single grower. The marketers turned a weakness into a perceived strength (they probably had experience in promoting blended whisky as something good).

I happen to know that the cider in question hasn't changed since it was largely confined to what we in the UK call 'winos', in its original home market – that is, homeless people who appear to survive solely on the nutritious content of high alcohol cider and lager. All that had changed was a major marketing campaign and rebranding effort.

This focus on alcohol promotion shouldn't be taken as an indication of any my own personal tastes. Actually, I find the area of addiction to be illuminating in the understanding of human weakness and decision-making. This is something we shall come back to in Part Two.

Anyway, back to the cloud. What is it? Very simply, it doesn't exist. It is a marketing term - perfectly chosen, as it is designed to hide the detail of what you are actually buying. Many systems have been rebranded over the last few years to be cloud services – just like the rebranded cider, nothing has changed, other than the badge.

In many cases, hosted service became "software as a service', which in turn evolved to 'on demand service', and then to 'cloud' services. Nothing changed, other than the marketing label.

It is worth thinking about some of the general characteristics that you usually find associated with a cloud-based service offering:

- Low cost – a key driver for moving services from your environment into the cloud is usually an overall cost reduction. Therefore, design decisions are often made to keep costs down, not to maximise security.

- Internet-facing – the providers' systems must be Internet-facing in order to deliver the service across the Internet. This exposes systems to constant probing by hackers.

- Web administration – a cost-effective way to give you administration access (usually just with a username and password). As with Internet banking (as still operated by the majority of banks), this simple access control mechanism is easily defeated by people with malicious intent.

- 'Efficient' support – often using outsourced support or support divisions in low-cost geographic locations. The systems administrators and support staff may be in a different organisation, in a different continent.

- Global – many providers are large with globally distributed systems. This introduces challenges in establishing common security standards and ongoing compliance.

- New – this field tends to be driven by new features and constant innovation. The main driver is to bring changes to the market, rather than to test them extensively for security weaknesses.

If you are familiar with IT security, you can see that each of the common features of cloud computing is also a strong warning sign of potential information security vulnerabilities.

It was of interest, therefore, when we received a client brief from a global cloud provider.

The Challenge

"Can you trick our service desk into giving you access as a customer?"

The request came with a very limited budget – not much more than a couple of days of my time.

This was one of those occasions when, under normal circumstances, I would have turned the assignment down. We work on the principle that smaller jobs usually don't give us the opportunity to work properly, and the client fee is unlikely to really cover the amount of time we put in – especially that unscheduled thinking time that is difficult to account for.

However, on this occasion, the request was from an existing client – I had previously helped develop some of their internal information security processes (although not their service desk procedures). So I felt some ownership of the account, and I like the information security manager. I do find that my personal preference for who to work with is taking an increasing prominence. This is largely due to the expanding team within ECSC giving me more opportunity to be selective in my own engagements. But please don't take it too personally if I decide not to be involved in your engagement. It might be just that I am too busy elsewhere.

As with many cloud providers, this company's customers had a web interface that gave them full administration access. For this service, that meant access to stored information as well as enabling the interception (or redirection) of confidential communication.

My challenge was to impersonate one of their customers, and call their service desk.

I was specifically barred from calling their customer as them, and tricking them into giving up their login and password details. This was, quite rightly, judged to be a little too easy. It is interesting that a global provider has a security system with a weakness that they don't even believe needs testing, because they perceive it as being so easy to breach.

The client instructed me as to which of their customers I had to pretend to be when I rang the service desk. They had obtained their customer's permission for this. This was sensible, and I would have recommended it anyway. There is always a risk that, during my testing, their service desk calls their customer back, and the customer then thinks they are under attack.

Having one customer give permission for me to impersonate them did allow the containment of this risk. In my experience, your customers are quite pleased to be involved in security testing – they find it interesting, and it does give them reassurance that you are taking your security seriously.

Thinking and Planning

So, where can I find out the vulnerabilities of the service desk operation? You can assume that there must be a procedure to either allocate a new administrator login and password, or just to reset an existing administrator login. These might be tightly defined procedures, or just established practice within a team. For a global organisation, I did expect formal procedures. Dealing with diverse geographic locations and cultures requires common processes.

One clue as to the vulnerabilities was that in their brief, the client included the fact that they had "strict security procedures" in place with regard to resetting passwords.

Now, I regard 'strict security procedures' as a vulnerability.

That is not a typo. Strict security procedures can, in many cases, be vulnerable to social engineering attack. Let me explain:

If you have procedures that are too strict, then they tend not to be able to take all circumstances into account. This is in contrast to 'flexible' security procedures that might be able to adapt more to a given threat.

In my experience, when operating under strict procedures, targets can often be exploited by simply taking them into a scenario that sits outside of the boundaries of (their understanding of) the existing procedures. As in this situation, if they don't have any guidance, they are more likely to follow my instructions. You will see how I used this technique as this adventure unfolds.

I also understood that the client had a globally dispersed 24/7 support arrangement. This is increasingly common. What is also common is that the further away you get from the corporate centre, the less influence the central information security function has. I intended to use this to my advantage.

Another factor with global companies is that different cultures will interpret security rules in different ways. Some cultures value following a hierarchy more than others, whereas some cultures expect more 'common sense' to be applied.

I clearly had constraints, not just in time, but also in the use of only one of their customers as an identity in my attack. My research uncovered a wealth of information about their customer:

1. They were an IT service company.

2. Their website detailed some of their personnel, including senior managers and engineers.

3. A search of the UK Companies House information revealed their last posted annual accounts and company information. This was useful in obtaining details of directors and company ownership – confirming that the managing director was also the principle owner.

However, I needed a pretext for my calls to the service desk – some reason for needing password resets, combined with a real need to bypass the existing security procedures. Clearly, what I required was some sort of emergency situation – and if this could happen overnight, it would give me a reason to call different service desk support centres (a useful attack strategy).

This testing took place during a UK recession, during the financial crisis that unfolded after 2008, and I realised I could use this to my advantage. So here was the scenario:

•   An overnight office move. This gave a reason for needing support through the night, and a valid context for making infrastructure changes. Moving IT equipment is always a little fraught, and a good reason why an organisation may need out-of-hours support. This scenario also gives a convenient reason why certain personnel (who might be the normal contacts) may not be available – hence the reason for requiring support.

- • Redundancies. If the office move was related to a general downsizing, then it could be happening at the time of redundancies. This gives another reason why key people are not available, and potentially why key administration logins need to be reset.

Attack Strategy

My overall strategy was to make a series of calls, first to the service desk in the UK, and then to others – probably the US and then the Far East.

Making a number of calls is a very basic social engineering technique, as multiple communications build trust. I have previously observed the way that we tend to build trust, and a belief in someone's identity, purely on the fact that we have communicated with them on a number of occasions.

An example of this is when we visit our clients for the first time, as part of a 'presale' process. A first visit can often be a little frustrating for our sales consultants, as the client doesn't really open up and give us enough information to be able to formulate a proper strategy to help them fully. However, by the second, third, or even fourth meeting, the communication changes completely – an effective sales consultant moves from stranger to best friend.

Many years ago, when I first got involved in this process, I was surprised at the shift that clients make – not only giving you new information in later visits, but often completely contradicting what they had said in the first meeting.

So, we tend to open up considerably as we get to know people. However, from a social engineering point of view, the trust we develop, and the fact that we now feel we 'know' the person, is purely based upon what they have told us.

When I debrief individual targets after social engineering testing, it is fascinating to hear how they describe giving away information to people they 'know'. However, when you track back where this belief came from, you understand that it was based solely on information supplied by the social engineer. So, after testing or a social engineering incident, you should not take the debriefing of the victims too literally, as there is a tendency for people to say what they think you want to hear – and they are often adding a conscious interpretation of actions that were subconsciously controlled.

Although this tendency to develop trust purely based on what someone tells you about themselves may sound illogical, it is actually a reasonable approach to developing relationships. When you think about the hundreds of people that we develop relationships with, the vast majority of them are genuine. A reasonable assumption to operate your life upon is that someone tells you the truth about who they are. This is why historically, fraudsters of all types are so successful – our society is not designed to detect people lying.

It would be most inconvenient if you had to perform a series of detailed, and independently verified, background checks on everyone you had any sort of communication with. Clearly, this approach is becoming more common for organisations recruiting personnel, but it is not (currently) feasible in everyday life. For historic reasons, and the reminders of less than desirable political systems, we don't like the idea of using identity cards and other sorts of authentication in everyday situations.

Therefore purely by having multiple communications, you can build up a trust and relationship with an individual. In the context of this attack, my trust was going to develop more at an organisational level, as my multiple calls were actually intended to be with different individuals (at different global support centres). Therefore, the trust and associated belief in my identity (or identities) with my targets was going to be developed through what I anticipated would be records within a Customer Relationship Management (CRM) system. If I could generate a realistic set of records from my calls, then a level of trust would be assumed by the next person that I targeted.

By increasing the level of trust, I intended to in effect 'escalate' my privileges within the system, towards my ultimate goal of administration level access. I was making an assumption that the global CRM system would be somewhat flawed in this regard.

Execution & Techniques

CALL ONE - 17:45 (UK SUPPORT)

I started the attack by calling as the managing director (CEO) of the customer organisation.

The time was important, as I knew (from the cloud provider website) that the UK Support Centre closed at 18:00. Therefore, I assumed that the support person would probably be thinking more about 'home time', and perhaps some managers might not be around for them to consult.

There is another reason why attacking someone at the end of a shift is a good idea – people are less engaged consciously when they are hungry. This is due to glucose depletion.

This was very nicely demonstrated with a study in the *Proceedings of the National Academy of Sciences* in the US in 2011. It studied the decisions of eight parole judges who spent their whole day reviewing applications for parole from prison. They get through lots of these (spending less than 10 minutes on each on average). Your chance of success in getting parole in front of them is only 35%.

Now, this is important, especially if you are reading this with the intention of putting your newfound social engineering skills to illegal use. Why you would do that is not clear, when there are so many exciting and very legal avenues for using social engineering.

Anyway, the study did a simple thing. It plotted the likelihood of a prisoner gaining a successful parole against the time since the judges had their last food break. Parole judges are a good subject for this, as their decision is easy to measure (yes/no) and they can't be sneaking snacks in open court.

You are probably thinking at this stage, "Yes, Ian, another of your examples of an extremely subtle effect". Well, you would be wrong.

The results of the study are far from subtle:

- Directly after eating, the judges awarded, on average, 65% of prisoners parole.

- In the period before they ate, the chances of gaining parole fell to near zero.

The moral? Don't break the law with your social engineering. If you do, don't get caught. (My experience is that only beginners and complete amateurs get caught). And, if caught, and you are up for parole, fake illness if you are due before lunch, so you can take the first slot after the meal break.

The conclusion that psychologists have come to is that when we are hungry, our conscious brain is less likely to get engaged. Instead, we rely on subconscious automated processes. In the case above, the default (automatic) decision is to turn down the parole. On the other hand, granting parole is a risky decision that takes considerable conscious processing.

Therefore, an attack at the end of the working day could have less risk that the target would actively, and consciously, engage in the process in a way that might lead them to become suspicious.

These sorts of assumptions might not be correct. After all, the call might be picked up by a manager who has just eaten a chocolate bar. But with experience, you find that you can usually be reasonably accurate with these assumptions and they help you plan accordingly. Of course, you don't make tactical decisions that rely on these assumptions being 100% correct. It is just that having a perceived scenario for what you will encounter can help you formulate your strategy.

My call was to prepare the ground for the later calls.

Firstly, I introduced myself, saying I was the MD, and that we were undertaking an office move through the night. I explained that, due to relocating the network, we would have to make some administration changes to the cloud service. The primary reason for my call was to find out if support was available through the night (I already knew it was).

These exploratory calls are useful, as they give you a chance to learn more and adapt your attack plans accordingly. The first call also gives me a first opportunity to assess the personality of a service desk operator. This could further inform my planning, as you often find similar personalities within an organisation – cultures tend to attract (and retain) like-minded individuals.

Personality Profile

Phone calls, being quite quick, sometimes don't give you enough evidence to reach firm conclusions on someone's personality – at least, not at a conscious level. You miss out on clues such as the way people dress, their general physical appearance, and also clues given from their eye movements. You can learn a lot from the way people speak – both in the words they choose and their tone of voice. Once you are fully proficient in this type of conscious analysis, you can move beyond this, and let your own subconscious inform you.

In these situations, you can just rely on your subconscious to picture the person sitting there in front of you and show you their personality (in effect, you trust your intuition, as this is your subconscious reading the clues).

Notice, in the sentence above, I use two visual words ('picture' and 'show'). This reflects my own dominant visual communication, and is also useful in communicating with the majority of the population that shares this tendency.

I might rewrite the sentence for a more auditory person as follows:

"In these situations, you can just rely on your subconscious to listen to the person sitting there in front of you – and you will literally hear their personality."

I'm sure you get the picture.

Actually, it would be much better to say, "This must be music to your ears."

Now, at this stage you might be thinking about people who are dominant Kinesthetics. You may have heard many people tell you to rely on your "gut feeling". Don't jump to the conclusion that they must be Kinaesthetic. You will actually find these people are in quite a small minority. Using the word "feeling" doesn't mean that they are within this group. Sometimes we use a variety of sense-related words or phrases, often because they are common terms. "Gut feeling" is one of these.

In some cases, you need to tap into a good segment of communication before you can reach a firm conclusion regarding someone's dominant sensory process.

Mind you, this is a good point to consider when you might rely on the 'instincts' that lead to a 'gut feeling':

A good rule of thumb is that when most people say this, they are talking uninformed rubbish. They notice the times their gut feeling worked, and forget the times it was wrong.

It reminds me of a colleague who used to quote the (rather bogus) concept of 'synchronicity' when I called him, as he had been thinking about me just a few minutes previously.

Was this a big surprise? Not really – I was his boss, and called him regularly throughout the working day.

What he failed to notice were the times he thought about someone and they didn't call him. I took a few minutes out to help him translate 'synchronicity' into 'coincidence'.

Yet I have just said that I can rely on my subconscious to give me a good 'feel' for someone on the phone. Why is my gut feeling more reliable than others'?

Simply, your gut feeling is the summation of your experience and expertise in similar situations. So, if like me, you have spent years studying people, and interact each month with hundreds of people in numerous organisations, then you should 'trust' these instincts.

You must decide if your subconscious has had a chance to acquire expertise in the area you are getting a 'gut feel' about.

> For instance, if on your first flying lesson, you get a 'gut' feeling that you are ready to fly solo, my best advice is to let your conscious (more logical) brain keep control, and wait for the instructor to arrive before you take off.

The service desk agent confirmed that we could obtain support through their 24/7 support desk, and confirmed that the same telephone number would route the call to the appropriate support desk. She also confirmed that each agent would be able to see the history of any previous calls.

I explained that I wasn't sure who would be available at my end to carry out the admin changes, and that we had also made some recent redundancies. I added that I wasn't sure who had access to the system. This gave a good pretext for needing to know details, and also why I couldn't find out the information for myself.

"I think John P will have access, but he isn't here on site yet".

I suspected John would have an account, as the customer's own website listed him as a senior engineer.

"Yes, I can see an account for John P", the agent confirmed.

The agent kindly explained that changes could only be made by a registered administrator. However, she offered to help in the following ways, as she:

1. Offered to e-mail me a list of who had access, and to what level.

2. Explained that in order to set up a new administration account, she would need official written management authorisation.

I accepted the first offer with one proviso, saying:

"Yes, that would be helpful. However, we've just shut down the exchange server in preparation for the move. Can you send the list to my Hotmail account please, as I can access that from my laptop?"

She duly obliged, and I gave her the Hotmail address I had prepared based on the name of the managing director.

So far, the 'strict procedures' hadn't caused me too much trouble. The agent was really just explaining how support worked, who could get support, and what the procedure was to create new administration accounts.

The procedures for new accounts gave some options, including authorisation on company headed paper, via fax.

I created a mock-up of a letterhead in case I needed that option. However, that wasn't my primary aim, as the service desk might keep a genuine copy on file for comparison (although in my experience, this is quite rare).

I thanked the lady for her help, and assured her that when John P arrived, we would probably be okay.

The first set of objectives had now been achieved:

1. Establish contact, and create a CRM record of this.

2. Communicate the pretext for requiring further support.

3. Extract information regarding who has a login.

4. Find out some details on the procedures for creating new administration logins.

Time for a quick break, and to think about the next call. I reviewed my planning notes and assessed what changes might be appropriate, based on the information gleaned in call one, and the personality I encountered.

CALL TWO - 20:30 (BST) (USA SUPPORT)

"Hello, this is John P from XXXX in the UK, I understand you can give us some support on reconfigurations we need to do this evening."

This was actually my opening line, repeated for the fourth time. I had discovered that the main obstacle to someone socially engineering the out-of-hours support service was that the service was terrible. This was an unintended layer of security protection.

I had been transferred four times, and kept waiting for over one hour, before I spoke to a person in a position to help me. There appeared to be some confusion over whether we were allowed out-of-hours support, and then as to whether I could be put through to an actual service engineer.

I decided that being annoyed, and frustrated, might be a realistic strategy. This was quite an easy role to play, as I was by this time starting to feel somewhat annoyed by the wait.

When I finally spoke to an engineer, I explained the situation, and said I had been kept waiting, and that my managing director was getting increasingly angry. I explained that he had spoken to UK support and they had promised an out-of-hours service.

The service engineer was very apologetic, and said:

"Yes, I can see you have a ticket open and that your managing director has arranged for support. How can I help?"

Psychological Techniques

In this case, my annoyance and frustration had the effect of helping the engineer to adopt a very compliant personality profile.

As I pushed my personality (Driver/Expressive) to the top of the matrix, he was (as an Analytical/Amiable) forced to the bottom.

This is a good example of where I change the personality position of the target. I don't particularly need to assess his natural personality that he adopts at work. Rather, I force him in the direction that suits my requirements for the attack.

"Thanks for understanding. We have an issue here, as due to the office move, our file servers are now in transit and the only logins we regularly use are stored there."

"Yes, I see your difficulty", he replied.

"I need to reconfigure the service with the new IP range for the new office".

Depending upon the cloud service you use, it is common to have a degree of integration with your office systems. In this case, having the IP address range configured on the service allowed for certain communication between the office and the cloud provider.

The impact of this change would be to allow me to intercept communications, and conduct what is referred to as a 'man in the middle' attack. This means that genuine communication would be sent to an address of my choice, and then I could relay it back to the original destination.

The beauty of this attack is that an attacker can intercept communication for an extended period of time without detection. The only indication to the customer that I was carrying out this interception would be the incorrect IP address setting in their configuration. This is likely to be a setting that they rarely change, and therefore could go undetected for an extended period of time.

The service engineer was most helpful: "Yes, I can change that for you now," he said.

A principle of social engineering testing is to minimise disruption to the client, and in this case to their customer (whom I was pretending to be). Any set up to intercept communication, and conduct an actual man in the middle attack, could be prone to error that might cause disruption.

Also, I had no need to actually intercept and view communication in order to prove that I could have done it, so I gracefully declined the help:

"Thanks, that is really helpful. I just need to ensure I have the right IP addresses – I don't want to break things. I'll call you back when I've double-checked that these are correct."

In terms of meeting the requirements of accessing confidential communication, the testing was successful. However, I still hadn't actually obtained a full administration login – and this would give further access to stored confidential information.

Also, I had not yet called the third global support centre. My suspicion was that this centre would be more 'distant' from the information security manager control, and therefore likely to be a good target for gaining full access.

In addition, I would now have more history recorded in the CRM system, showing that the situation was 'genuine'.

CALL THREE - 06:00 (BST) ('FAR EAST' SUPPORT)

I have not named the country involved here. This is partly to reduce the chances of anyone correctly identifying the cloud provider in question.

In addition, it turned out that the information security manager didn't actually know which country provided support at this time. In my pretesting briefing, he said it was one country. However, when I made my third call, and asked the engineer where he was based, it was somewhere else.

This confirmed my suspicion that this support centre was quite detached from the control of the UK-based information security team.

My strategy on call three was simple, and emergency that needed full access immediately.

Calling as John P, the engineer, I said:

"If I don't get this sorted immediately, my managing director is going to fire me. He's already very angry about the delays we had in getting through to someone in the US support centre last night."

I expected that I would have to deliver some sort of management authorisation, in line with the previously disclosed 'strict procedures'. However, I was pleasantly surprised when the engineer quickly responded:

"Yes, I can see we have been helping you, and that you have had some difficulties. Would you like me to reset your login with a new password?"

"Yes, that would be fine", I responded, and proceeded to take down the details of the new login and password.

Personality Profile

Sometimes you don't care about the personality of your target. This chap was just so helpful, and gave me all the help I needed immediately. There was not much time to do an analysis, and not much need.

I could use some deductive reasoning to show that he was Analytical and Amiable, which was pretty obvious for a helpdesk operator. However, his communication was just too quick – there was definitely a Driver in there. I would therefore suggest that this was a relatively young man, who wouldn't be in this role very long.

In these situations where you get rapid compliance, there is no need for complex analysis. Just keep to the minimalist strategy and just carry out your prepared plan of attack.

I knew the login name was an e-mail address, as this had been communicated to my Hotmail account during the first call.

Not needing to access confidential information, I logged in once in order to generate a screen shot for my report, and then logged out immediately.

I placed a call to the information security manager, to give him details of the account, so he could arrange for it to be disabled. I then proceeded to write up my notes ready for my report presentation later that day. Yes, my job does involved lots of writing of reports – it is not all fun and games!

I also sent a quick e-mail to my colleagues who were simultaneously conducting penetration testing for the same client, declaring myself the winner of our little 'who gets full access first' competition. The fact that they were not due on site to start until 9 a.m. that day had helped me somewhat in my victory.

Results & Analysis

Full administration access in only three phone calls, using nothing more than publicly available information about one of the users of the cloud service, represented a major social engineering vulnerability, and highlights the inherent weaknesses involved in cloud-based services. I have no doubt that this sort of attack could be replicated for the majority of cloud service providers.

Remember, at no time, in any call, had an attempt been made to authenticate the identity of the caller. As the three calls proceeded, the engineers were assuming identification, based on a (really quite short) call history.

The main strategy deployed here was the gradual escalation of privileges and requests for information and access. None of the requests appeared to be a big enough jump for the service desk staff to feel the need to carry out an authentication.

The disclosure of the 'strict' security procedures could not really be classed as a weakness, as you have to communicate procedures to your clients if you expect them to follow them.

However, sending me full account details, to a new Hotmail account, was disclosing information that should have been regarded as confidential. Remember, at that point, I had not been through any sort of authentication.

If you take the final call in isolation, it looks like a clear breach of rules – a password reset without proper authentication. Reading the procedures that should have been followed, it certainly seemed that way.

However, to the engineer, does this mean authenticating every caller at every stage? Clearly not, as we tend to authenticate people at the start of a support session. Therefore, does the engineer need to re-authenticate each call, or just the first call? In this case, the identity was assumed, based on the information supplied by the CRM solution.

Remember, your customers will get annoyed if they have to repeatedly re-authenticate each time they speak to someone new. Security protection has to be smart, but also not too intrusive. Testing shows you if you have the balance right.

Get Through Our Secure Logins

Introduction

I used to be involved in securing UK government systems (I will have to shoot you now that you know that). In many cases, these 'highly secure' systems needed to be truly 'air gapped' with the Internet and wider communications networks. This means no connectivity to any other networks, not even through tightly controlled firewalls and two-factor authentication. This high level of segregation ensures that a security breach can only come through direct physical access to systems (this assumes that systems architects and administrators follow the rules – and in many cases, they either don't understand the rules, or find them too restrictive).

This extreme level of network security doesn't prevent a wide range of electronic sniffing from the perimeter of the location, but that's a topic that's beyond the scope of our discussion into human weaknesses.

In the commercial environment, it is increasingly common to expect systems to be open to the world. This is clearly essential if you want to offer services across the internet – a very typical requirement today. So what do you do if you need to deliver the highest levels of security, and you need open access to a large number of individual clients?

If you are an information security professional, you might be thinking, "Give them two-factor authenticated access" – usually meaning a hardware token to supplement a username and password. However, if you have many thousands of users, who might not need to access the system very often, this sort of solution can be too expensive and seen by users as being awkward.

This just leaves you with the 'normal' website type security controls.

So how do you deliver a greater level of security for a critical, web-facing, application that gives users access to highly confidential details of their financial management – and the ability to move their funds? These funds can be in the tens or hundreds of thousands of pounds sterling.

This brings us to our next adventure – how to gain access to a financial management system open to thousands of individual investors. This was clearly very critical, and therefore the client had implemented a 'very secure' login system.

Knowing that a simple username and password would be too easy to break, the client required a number of different authentication details, including:

- An account number

- A password

- Date of birth

The client perceived this as demonstrating greater security than a typical login, needing three different pieces of information.

In addition, a record was kept on the central system of the clients' mothers' maiden names – to be used as a further authentication check when giving telephone support to someone who might have forgotten their password.

For those international readers not familiar with mother's 'maiden' name, this is your mother's surname (or family) name before she gets married. The use of this for authentication is quite common in a number of countries, and relies on a few assumptions:

1. You are from a culture where you have a family name.

2. Your mother changed her surname to that of your father.

3. That somehow this information is secret.

Clearly, these are quite important assumptions, with an increasing number of occasions where they don't apply.

However, assuming that the mother's maiden name will work (after all, the user can supply any name for this when they sign up), this gives a total of four independent pieces of information required to gain access to the system, and therefore a nice, meaty social engineering challenge.

We were also assured that the people who controlled access, and critically reset authentication details, were very well trained and the 'strongest link' in the client's security chain.

However, there is an often-overlooked aspect of having a perceived increase in security, which is that it can give users a false sense of how secure a system is. In the same way as barrier entry systems make people believe that anyone on the inside must be trusted, extensive authentication details can make people believe the systems cannot be cracked. This can lead to them relaxing their guard – and this can be the start of a social engineering approach to finding weaknesses.

If you know that a given piece of information is all that is needed to gain access, then you know to protect it. However, if you think each piece is only part of the required information, you might not protect it to the same level.

We see this as a weakness in the common 'defence in depth' strategy. Although this is a good idea, it often means that each layer of security isn't quite strong enough, as the further layers are assumed to compensate. Clearly, if each layer has a weakness, there is a route to a breach.

Another interesting feature of this adventure is to allow us to examine just how secret personal information, such as date of birth and mother's maiden name, actually is.

The Challenge

As is often the case in these types of engagement, the client insisted that we could not target their customers. This is definitely the easy route:

1. Contact customers pretending to be our client's helpdesk.

2. Alert them to a security issue, such as someone logging into their account from another country and transferring funds.

3. Offer them a solution – in particular, say that they are 'protected' if they act now.

4. Take them 'through security'.

Of course, step four is the attack – it gives you a chance to gain access to their confidential information. In the case of this system, I would get them to confirm their account number, date of birth and mother's maiden name.

These details would then be used to attack the client's helpdesk and perform a password reset.

Remember, this route was not allowed by the client, as it was judged to be too easy. It's interesting, again, that a system is set up with a major known vulnerability, judged to be easy to exploit, and nothing is done to counter this threat.

Anyway, back to our challenge. We had to obtain a password reset for a sample of users. These users were the executives of selected customers of our client. All we had as our starting point for our attack identities were the names of their customers and the senior executives to be impersonated.

We could see the system online, and knew it needed the three pieces of information (account number, date of birth, and password) to log in. Remember, the client told us that their helpdesk procedures were very tight, and required someone's mother's maiden name in order to perform a password reset.

So, breaking each of these down:

- Account number - known by customer, and needed to access support.

- Date of birth – known by the customer, and not given out by the client (they have no need to).

- Mother's maiden name, also known by the customer, and again, not given out by the client as part of any support call.

- Password – can be reset by the helpdesk, but only by being given the three pieces of information above.

So, time to do some thinking....

Thinking and Planning

For this exercise, I was joined by Shaun, one of our consultants at ECSC. Shaun has some excellent attributes as a social engineer: he has a very analytical brain, but is also quick thinking and decisive. It's a useful skill combination for social engineering, particularly over the phone.

The attack strategy was simple: to obtain all the required authentication details, except the password, and then use these to obtain a password reset from the helpdesk. Then we would have full access. Simple.

Our first task was to do some research on the individual customers we were to call as. The first challenge we set ourselves was very easy: date of birth. As each target individual was an executive of a customer, they had records at Companies House, including their name, address and date of birth.

So our four factors of authentication had just been reduced to three. This meant 25% towards our targeted information in the first few minutes of planning.

We suspected that we could obtain the account numbers quite easily. As you needed two additional pieces of 'secure' information in order to login, we determined that the helpdesk probably wouldn't regard the account number as being too confidential.

We also suspected that there might be some sort of 'emergency' procedure that we might be able to activate and exploit. As this would probably require the use of a fax, we seconded one of our support staff to customise our outgoing fax machine. If we were to send fake faxes, we wouldn't want it to say ECSC Ltd in the header. So we informed our own service desk that we might require some quick editing of our outgoing fax settings. They were only too pleased to assist.

Attack Strategy

For our attacks, we decided to adopt two different strategies. Mine was to try and trick the helpdesk into giving me my own mother's maiden name. Yes, you heard that correctly.

Shaun decided to take a different angle. He thought he might be able to find out some others' mother's maiden names.

Execution & Techniques

Let's start with the account numbers. This involved a rather simple call:

"Hello, my name is John Smith, I am the managing director of XXXX. I wonder if you can help me. We are making a number of redundancies here this week. I understand that some of them will have logins with the ClientSystemYY, so I will need to have some of these disabled later in the week."

"Yes, let me take a look. Do you have your account number?"

"No, I'm not even sure if I have a login. My secretary deals with this sort of thing normally, but I don't want her to know about the redundancies."

"Okay, can you tell me the company name again?"

"Yes, it's XXXX, based in London."

"Oh yes, I can see you have about 20 accounts live."

Personality Profile

If you have been practicing your profiling by listening to key words to indicate the mode of communication, you will have seen this agent use 'tell me' and 'I can see' in their first two responses.

Does this mean they are visual or auditory?

Actually, neither – you can't always take every instance of these words as a definitive pointer to the way someone thinks. After all, a phone operator has to request you to 'tell' them information, and will be 'seeing' results on their screen. Sometimes these words just occur naturally and have no special significance.

Therefore, don't jump to early conclusions. Listen to more

communication and look for patterns. You should especially be on the 'look out' for words that are an optional communication description.

So, if you are explaining something, you might expect this reaction:

"Yes, I see what you mean".

However, an alternative reaction of:

"Yes, I'm getting a feel for this now", could strike you as somewhat unusual.

(If you are kinaesthetic, you will not 'feel' that the last response was in any way unusual.)

Remember, the words are only one piece of evidence. For telephone communication, tone and pace of speech are just as big a clue.

For most of these types of interactions, simply matching the pace of the other speaker can be a good means of aligning your communication.

Psychological Techniques

You might be thinking that the process above sounds (or looks?) a bit complex. You don't have to worry yourself, as there is a good shortcut to matching their personality – simply mimic their tone of voice and (importantly) the speed of their communication. This will help your communication automatically match their preferred style.

This is similar to the example I gave in *Hacking the Human* of bypassing the whole area of body language matching, and instead, just allowing your breathing rate to match that of your target. (Clearly, this is only applicable face-to-face. Oh, and remember to get their breathing rate from watching shoulder movements, not

> staring at their chest!
>
> Because we all have the potential to adapt our personality profiles, in different situations, you can become quite adept at matching another person's style without too much prompting or conscious manipulation of your state.

Back to my first discussion:

"Okay, that's fine, some of these will need disabling – how do I do that?"

"Well, it needs to be an administrator who does that."

"Okay, are you able to tell me who is an administrator?"

"Yes, you have four at the moment, would you like me to tell you who they are?"

"Yes, that would be helpful."

"Okay, would you like these e-mailed to you?"

"No, just give me them over the phone. My e-mail is handled by my secretary, and I don't really want her to see this."

"Okay, if you have a pen, I'll give you the details. Would you like to know who has the normal user accounts, as well?"

"Yes, that would be helpful."

The helpdesk agent then proceeded to read out the list of users, and critically, he included the account numbers, as he said:

"You will need the account numbers for changes to accounts, so I'll give you those."

This confirmed our suspicion that account numbers would not be regarded as too confidential.

I also tried a variation on this approach with the next call to a different helpdesk agent:

"Hello, my name is John Smith, I'm the managing director of XXXX. I wonder if you can help me. We're making a number of redundancies here this week. I understand that some of them will have logins with the ClientSystemYY.

"I need to access the system to see who has an account. I have a note of my password, and know that I need my date of birth, but I can't seem to find my account number."

This also led to the same result, although only a single account number this time.

A third variation happened when I called asking for my own account number (using the pretext above), and the agent volunteered the full list of users, along with their account numbers. In this case, I tried another variation, to see if their procedures allowed for non-work e-mail communication.

"Yes, can you please e-mail this to me? But my secretary sees all my e-mail, and she mustn't know about the redundancies, so can you forward them to my Gmail account?"

The agent duly obliged.

This gave us another piece of the jigsaw. We were now at 50% of the details required. Armed with the account numbers and dates of birth, we could call the helpdesk for a password reset – but we still knew we needed the magic mother's maiden name.

"Hello, I am John Smith from XXXX."

"Good afternoon, Mr Smith, may I have your account number?"

"Yes, it's 123456789."

"Thank you, how may I be of assistance?"

"I haven't used my account for quite a while, and I don't seem to have a record of my password. Can you give me a new one?"

"Yes, I can do a password reset for you.

Can I take your mother's maiden name?"

"No, I'm not sure what I used."

"Sorry, I don't understand."

"Well, I use different mother's maiden names for different logins, as I don't think using the same one is a good idea. I don't have a record of what I used for this one."

"Oh I see, well I need to have that information before I can do a password reset. Why don't you try a few that you've used before, and I'll tell you if any are correct."

Interesting concept – repeated attempts with feedback from the operator. This starts to look like a brute force mother's maiden name attack. However, I suspected the agent would start to be suspicious if I started to read hundreds of names.

"I'm not sure I really want to read you out the list of typical names I use."

Now this may look like a failure. However, I had established a valid reason for not knowing my own mother's maiden name - therefore, the helpdesk agent now had a problem to solve. I tried a different route:

"What can I do to reset the account?"

"We'll need signed authorisation on company headed paper. If you can fax that through to me, I can reset the password."

Ah ha! The emergency procedure. Everyone has one – and if they don't, you can often get one invented just for you.

I spent a few minutes constructing a fake headed paper, and a request was written, signed and despatched. A call five minutes later confirmed receipt, and a password reset was performed.

In trying a number of similar approaches, I also encountered this interesting, and somewhat amusing variation:

I had obtained my account number, so rang the helpdesk with an intended similar strategy of having used a now forgotten mother's maiden name. However, in this case, the agent came back with an interesting reply:

"I don't think this account has ever been set up. There is no date of birth or mother's maiden name set."

"Oh, that is strange. Do you want me to give you them now?"

"No, I can't do that."

Well it was worth a try!

"You'll have to fax them to me."

"Okay, and if I then call you back, will you be able to give me a password?"

"Yes, I can do that." I prepared another fax, this time with my date of birth and mother's maiden name on it. I then called the helpdesk back, and was immediately put through to the same person.

"Hello, this is John Smith, we spoke about 15 minutes ago. Did you get my fax?"

"Yes, Sir. I have updated your details. Would you like me to set you a password?"

"Yes, please."

"Okay, I just need to take you through security."

I guessed what was coming next, but just to be sure, I asked:

"Oh, are you going to ask me for the details that I just sent you?"

"Yes, is that okay?"

"Yes, fine."

I had to smile.

Shaun's strategy was a little different. Having thought a little more about the information we had, he came up with a conjecture:

We already knew the names, addresses and dates of birth of a number of directors of businesses. It is reasonable to assume that at least some of them had not moved from the area of their birth. Therefore, assuming they had the same surname as their fathers and knowing their dates of birth, why not look at birth records to find out their mother's maiden names?

This strategy is now becoming less resource-intensive, as many birth records are now available online.

Results & Analysis

Sure enough, within a couple of attempts Shaun managed to find a number of relevant birth records that looked quite promising.

A call to the helpdesk confirmed the strategy and passwords were duly reset.

For the accounts that hadn't already been reset, and armed with the dates of birth,account numbers and mother's maiden names, we could conduct password resets with a single call.

So we had access to a 'secure' system that needed four pieces of information. Why did what should have been a secure online system only take a few phone calls (and fake faxes) to breach?

Firstly, the helpdesk clearly didn't regard the account number as being particularly confidential. This was not a surprise to us – in fact, we assumed it. As you add multiple layers of security, users start to perceive each individual one as being less important, even though the designers probably wouldn't agree with this.

Secondly, it turns out that both date of birth and mother's maiden name are not nearly as secret and secure as you might at first think.

If our targets had been younger, we would likely have incorporated the use of social media. Think about how many people post the details of their birthdays and ages online – meaning dates of birth are easily calculated. Some social media sites even invite you to add your date of birth to your public profile. In addition, with relationships viewable online, finding someone's mother is quite easy: if she either includes details of her parents, or still uses her original surname, then the mother's maiden name is easily obtained.

Thus, we have a system that requires four pieces of authentication information, and, armed with three of them, you can obtain the fourth through a password reset.

The fundamentals of the security architecture, and its assumptions regarding the confidentiality of certain pieces of personal information, were clearly flawed.

Also, the client didn't help by having helpdesk processes that allowed elements of the personal authentication information to be given out.

The client accepted signed headed paper without any reference to previously stored examples (either of the paper or the signature). You would be right in thinking that people sometimes change the design of headed paper, but it would still be a major improvement on accepting my homemade examples. Still, obtaining someone's genuine headed paper isn't a challenge – just write to them, and wait for an example to come back through the post. They usually add a signature for good measure.

Asking me for the authentication details I had just sent them was quite amusing. How can this be explained?

The helpdesk agent simply had no process for what to do if the authentication details in the system were blank. Therefore, he adapted the processes he did have (accepting a fax authorisation) to fill in the gaps in the helpdesk system. After that, my call back with the very same details was simply normal process.

What, then, is the solution?

This is a classic case of functionality against security. Having an online administration system with lots of users means that authentication needs to be efficient and cost-effective.

How many pieces of really secure information can a user be expected to remember? However, in this case, it was clear that the combination of the security mechanisms and helpdesk processes amounted to a relatively easy target.

There was scope for the redesign of process – something that we often help our clients achieve. As the attackers, we are usually the best people to evaluate options and design better processes. Many clients like this support. Others like to use us purely for our testing ingenuity.

Would I recommend some sort of hardware token two-factor authentication here? Actually, I think that would make sense – particularly looking at the value of the target. At least it could be offered as a costed option to customers. Then, if they refused, it could be taken that they were accepting some responsibility for security weaknesses. This would also serve to protect the customers from a social engineer targeting them directly for their authentication credentials.

In the future, we will most likely have some biometric solutions, but we certainly aren't there yet. For now, you must think about the systems you present to the Internet, what information is required, and just how confidential the personal information you utilise is in the process. Then examine your helpdesk procedures from the perspective of the social engineer. Or even better, get us to test them and show you the weaknesses.

An Inspector Calls

Introduction

Having highlighted remote social engineering in the last chapter, we are now back to on site exploits - a great challenge, and usually full of interesting nuances due to the face-to-face manipulation required.

It is great for the social engineer to be able to observe people, especially as they have to deal with unexpected circumstances.

Many organisations are now expected to develop and maintain secure sites, with physical entry controls that exceed the levels that you would expect in a typical business facility. This can be for genuine security threats, or in many cases just to satisfy the expectations of their customers.

This is an important aspect of security. You might not ever have detected a breach, or perceive the threat to be very large. However, if you aspire to serve large companies, then you need to meet, and hopefully exceed, their security requirements. It is worth remembering that a big multinational customer will have facilities in many countries, with greatly varying security environments. In addition, a large organisation will probably have a greater chance of suffering a breach somewhere, so they will be acutely aware of the risks.

In addition to designing a secure perimeter for secure sites, you will often find additional secure areas within their normal security perimeter – areas that have even tighter security controls in order to control access. This adventure is concerned with one such facility.

Another feature of this type of challenge is the lack of information, meaning we would be simulating a true 'zero knowledge' attack. Other than knowing that our target existed, and was located within a secure area, we didn't know any specific details regarding the actual security countermeasures.

This raises an important issue if you commission social engineering testing: how much do you tell the testers?

There are two extremes:

1. Don't tell them anything. This approach is designed to simulate a real attack. However, in practise it offers two drawbacks: i) In many cases, real breaches have some element of inside knowledge. ii) It is more costly in terms of testing time, as you need to build in a reasonable amount of research and surveillance activity in order to make the test realistic.

2. Give them extensive 'insider' knowledge, and highlight all the suspected vulnerabilities. This can have the benefit of reducing time (and cost) doing investigations and surveillance activities. However, it risks giving too much direction, so the testing offers little more than confirmation of known weaknesses.

The reality is that most engagements fall somewhere in the middle. The client will give us some idea of perceived weaknesses, but also be interested in the outcome of our own investigations and surveillance activities.

In this case, our client's challenge was firmly in the first category. We knew the site existed, what it did, and that a secure area was located somewhere within. And that was it.

How do you prepare for the unknown? I find two principles apply:

1. Guess. That means have a working conjecture, based on your experience, of what you are likely to find. In many cases, you will find that this gives you a reasonable starting point.

2. Be flexible. Have a plan that can be adaptable, and gives you scope to change. Combine this with an expectation that you will have to change your plans. Thinking on your feet is what often makes on-site social engineering so much fun.

The Challenge

"Gain access to our secure facility, and then remove some equipment from the secure caged storage area."

Here was another quite short and simple brief. However, we knew little of the facility, the security controls, or even the internal layout.

What we were told was that the client handled IT equipment, including equipment storing highly confidential information. As part of this process, equipment that needed to be stored for any period was placed in a secure caged area within the overall secure facility.

That is about the sum total of the intelligence we had regarding the operation. The site didn't really facilitate much surveillance activity, and the budget didn't make provision for it.

It was an interesting challenge for a social engineer.

Thinking and Planning

I needed a pretext for the attack, and to create a scenario that would allow me to access all areas, and be flexible enough to respond to the circumstances and challenges that I met.

A quick brainstorm with ECSC colleagues led to an idea: a Health and Safety Executive (HSE) Inspection.

Within the UK, the HSE have an important role to ensure safety in the workplace, and with that roles comes important rights. Critically, they:

1. Can make unannounced inspections.

2. Have a statutory right to entry, and movement within the organisation.

3. Can shut an operation down if they consider it unsafe.

This pretext gives a social engineer a number of advantages, both in gaining access and flexibility on site.

I had not used this particular pretext before, so did some quick research, and found another interesting feature of an HSE inspection: the inspector can insist upon access to employees without management being present. This is so that management do not answer the questions on behalf of employees, and also gives employees the opportunity to raise concerns with a level of confidentiality.

Clearly, an inspector would be viewed by most people as an authority figure, and this can be useful in a social engineering scenario.

Our research also quickly identified that the HSE very helpfully place a variety of forms that they use online. This enabled us to create some realistic documentation to use during the inspection.

We also created some other resources, including business cards and identity badges. As is usually the case, we didn't try to match these to genuine ones, as it is extremely unlikely that the client would know the precise details of an exact replica.

I did once have a client make a direct comparison, as he had a genuine business card from a large auditing organisation that I was pretending to be from on his desk. This wasn't during the testing, but during the feedback meeting. Interestingly, my fake was an almost exact copy, even though I had nothing to hand to copy. It just shows that business card designs for professional service organisations are so conservative that they are easily guessable, and rarely checked by anyone.

The final piece of my identity as an inspector was the appropriate high-visibility jacket. Thanks to the help of a friendly local screen printer, this came with a nice new HSE logo.

The nice thing about having logos and badges on lanyards etc, is that you often don't really need to introduce yourself. In many cases, you can just say, "I am here to do an inspection," and the surrounding identity gives the target the correct context.

Now, on to the attack.

Attack Strategy

I decided on an early morning start, primarily to be able to launch the inspection before any managers arrived. I wasn't sure if the business would be a full 24/7 operation – however, I assumed that deliveries would start quite early. Therefore, I parked up and approached the rear of the facility in search of a delivery bay area.

I was armed with my high-visibility jacket (creased and dusted up a little to look reasonably well worn), badge, clipboard, and a small portable camera to record my findings. It seemed reasonable that an inspector would take photographic evidence, and this also allowed me to photograph any specific vulnerabilities that I encountered, to be included in my report.

The effect that taking pictures can have is fascinating – and in many cases, the bigger the camera, the better. People taking photos in a very overt way are often given legitimacy by the observer, since logic tells them that anything suspicious would be done more covertly.

In this case, I took the opportunity to further enhance my look. Firstly, I selected a rather old suit – one that predated my recent fitness activities, and was a little large. In addition, as I was working out of the office for a few days (a rare occurrence) prior to the testing, I grew a beard. This all contributed to the look of an inspector. This might be a prejudicial view of what an inspector may look like, but it was a view likely to be shared by my targets.

I also had a shoulder bag. This was empty, ready to extract my target IT equipment.

Remember, I had no time for surveillance activities, so knew nothing of the layout of the facility.

Execution & Techniques

Approaching the loading bay, I could see that it was internally caged off, segregating deliveries from the internal facility – a sign that security was being taken seriously.

Rather than approach any individual, I simply entered the facility and proceeded to wander around, making a few notes on the HSE-branded forms on my clipboard.

It didn't take long for someone to ask, "Can I help you?"

Personality Profile

A young man working in a warehouse-type operation? Not likely to be a Driver personality (no puns necessary, given that we were next to a forklift truck).

Actually, I might have thought Amiable as a starting point. However, this young man had an impressive physique, with lots of attention paid to his general grooming. So, although he was still firmly to the right of our personality matrix, I had him moving into Expressive.

You can tell a lot from someone by the eyes. I don't just mean by following the NLP eye movement guide, although this can be very useful. In this case, our target had a vague 'is anybody really at home' look. This shows a level of conscious disengagement, and indicates a subconscious dominance to decision-making and actions.

You can get the 'feeling' about personality from just meeting someone. This is your subconscious making an instant assessment on your behalf. If you want to do this analysis consciously, then you can look at the relative pupil dilation of your target for the amount of ambient light. Pupils dilate as you become more consciously engaged. As pupil dilation also indicates attraction, it does make people that are more consciously engaged more attractive.

However, in this case, I let my subconscious do the analysis for me. This told me he was very unlikely to apply any analytical thought to the situation, and would simply accept what I told him.

Psychological Techniques

With an Amiable, I might instruct them in quite a reassuring way, keeping them in their relative comfort zone. However, with more of an Expressive, I will likely be more forceful – and in particular, speed up my communication somewhat, and be more assertive.

"Yes, thank you. I'm here to do a Health and Safety Inspection. You must let your supervisor know, as you need to get someone to accompany me through the facility."

Within a few minutes, the shift supervisor appeared and introduced himself.

Personality Profile

The shift supervisor was an interesting character: quite forceful, although a little too fancily dressed for his role – his suit was a little too sharp.

I pinned him high up between Expressive and Driver. His eyes said 'quite engaged' and critical, although his Expressive tendencies might indicate his focus would be more on looking good to his colleagues, rather then achieving serious organisational goals.

His questioning was a little superficial, not really indicating any real desire to understand the situation – more just to demonstrate his position of authority.

Expressives like to look good, and aim to enforce this personal view on everyone around them. They are most likely to be devious, and are probably the least trustworthy of the personalities in the matrix. They do not generally sit well within organisations.

Psychological Techniques

My approach with this person was similar – although rather than trying to dominate, I decided to treat him more as an equal, respecting his need to show his superiority.

Therefore, I tended to talk as if he already knew what I was doing, implying that I merely had to remind him of the process out of courtesy.

What you are doing is getting your own way, but leaving the person with the continued belief that they are in control of the situation.

I explained that this was an unannounced visit, and quite routine. I said there wasn't any particular concern or reported incidents, so it shouldn't take too long.

Previously, I had identified a risk connected with this exercise: I might inadvertently give out health and safety-related advice – and be wrong! This could be quite serious. Imagine a scenario where I declare an activity to be fine, and someone is injured (or worse) the next day carrying out that activity.

This sort of analysis is part of our general risk identification activity that goes with any social engineering testing engagement.

So, I had decided to invent a new HSE inspection rule, namely: "I will not give any advice or guidance during the inspection. That will come later, with my summary report and feedback to management."

I proceeded to ask about different areas of the business. Clearly, the operation involved the movement of goods, sometimes in large cases or pallets. Therefore, it was quite evident where health and safety issues might become apparent.

As I was being shown around, I simply asked about the safety features of each part of the operation, and made diligent notes on my pad. This allowed me to 'inspect' each area of the business and follow the flow of equipment through the operation.

It didn't take too long before the Health and Safety Manager appeared on the scene – apparently, she had been alerted and had come immediately to find me.

I explained the process, and said I had no reason to believe there was a problem and that the inspection was quite routine. I did tell her that there was a requirement for me to be left alone with the employees. I said that I would send for her if she was needed, and we would meet in due course for my feedback.

I was now successfully through the perimeter defences, and interacting with the business. It looked as if the scenario/pretext and my assumed identity were working successfully. However, I still hadn't accessed anything confidential – and certainly didn't have any equipment in my possession. It was time to create an opportunity.

As I had navigated the operation, I had quite quickly identified the secure caged area. I didn't make a beeline for it, as that might be a little too obvious. However, I made sure that we ended up near this part of the operation, so I could ask about its purpose.

It was pointed out that the person accompanying me had no access to this area, so I suggested that they hand me over to someone in the relevant team.

This handover, as we have seen in previous adventures, creates a strong authentication. The person to whom I am introduced may well believe the inspection is a planned activity, as I am simply introduced as, "Here is Ian, he's conducting a Health and Safety Inspection, and needs to ask you a few questions."

I could tell immediately that my new contact, an IT engineer, was quite easy to manipulate, and that this would probably be my best chance.

Personality Profile

This chap was a classic Amiable, although he appeared to be working in an IT role where I would expect to meet quite a few Analyticals. Therefore, I had him low down in the personality profile matrix, probably midway between Analytical and Amiable.

I briefly interacted with a colleague who was much more suited to the IT role: firmly Analytical, but with more Driver personality mixed in. He quizzed me in such a way that I knew he was not a good candidate for tricking into breaking rules in this context.

Psychological Techniques

So, I engineered my conversation back to Mr Amiable, so I could continue my manipulation of the inspection.

As previously stated, you need to keep Amiables in their comfort zone, so don't be too forceful, and help them to understand what is happening. Otherwise, there is a danger that they will pass you over to someone less compliant.

Just remember to make friends with Amiables. Most of their life is centred around friendship relationships, and this is very important to them.

It is one of the factors that emerges from a line drawn diagonally from the extreme Driver down to the extreme Amiable, and it can be a good guide to the size of someone's population of friends. Amiables will tend to have lots of friends, and extreme drivers will have very few (if any). The extreme Driver might have lots of colleagues and acquaintances, or business contacts, but not a reliance on deep friendships.

It was also still quite early in the morning, so not many employees were in the building. Therefore, I engineered the inspection to take us into the caged area. My new friend was only too pleased to help.

I then simply said:

"I need to see the relevant risk assessments for this area whilst I am here, can you please go and get Janet. She knows I am here, and knows she might be called. You can leave me here."

As soon as he left, I swiftly placed a piece of IT equipment in my bag.

When the Health and Safety Manager arrived, I simply said: "I think I can now look at your risk assessments. I want to start with this area, but we can go to your office if you prefer."

Janet then took me through her paperwork.

I thanked her, and praised their approach, and compared them with other inspections. I pointed out that I didn't have much time, as I was visiting another organisation that I would probably be shutting down, due to repeated health and safety failings.

Personality Profile

Janet was an interesting mix. If anything, I had her dead centre in the personality matrix.

This is an interesting position, as someone here might be able to move into each role as they need to, given their environment. A true personality chameleon can be a powerful personality: typically a very high achiever, who also enjoys a rich and varied life. The classic Renaissance (wo)man' or even, in extreme situations, a true polymath.

However, in Janet's case, as our conversation developed, I realised she wasn't in the centre in a flexible, can flip in any direction as required sense, but was rather 'stuck' in the middle.

I had the impression that she wouldn't be particularly effective; a sort of middle of the road manager, who doesn't really excel in any capacity. Harsh, perhaps, but the role of the social engineer is to analyse, make assumptions and exploit vulnerabilities.

The more extreme personalities can be useful in an organisation, as a team tends to be capable of higher performance if it has a mix of personalities. This assumes that the team can be managed effectively to bring out the best in each individual. Extreme personalities are also more fun for the social engineer, as it allows us to use a wider variety of techniques.

Psychological Techniques

What do you do with such a middle of the road personality? Actually, not a lot. As they don't have any extreme tendencies, you don't need to, either. Therefore, I tend to just play the middle of the road Mr Average.

Janet was very pleased to hear that she was doing such a good job, and I received her thanks before leaving.

Having left the site, I photographed the equipment for my report, and then came back to debrief the information security manager – and, of course, promptly return the equipment.

My report would be written and delivered the same day.

Results & Analysis

So, yet again, I had achieved unauthenticated access to all areas. In this case, that included the 'secure' caged area, and the target of removing confidential IT equipment.

My subsequent analysis with the information security manager was quite interesting. They had quite a mature information security system, fully certified to ISO 27001. These procedures clearly included the provision that all visitors had to be escorted at all times. The rules regarding the secure caged area reiterated these same provisions.

Why, then, did the employee leave a visitor in the caged area?

It's an interesting question, as he clearly understood the rule that all visitors had to be escorted at all times. Therefore, this requires a little thought. It's clear that if such rules are not obeyed, then the fundamentals of information security are broken, and the social engineer's goal is made much easier.

To start with, you need to consider what a rule is, and how we actually interpret them.

Let's take driving at excessive speed on the public highway as an example. Most people agree with the need for the rule, yet the vast majority of drivers break this same rule. Is this about getting caught, or is it that we choose to interpret when to abide by rules and when not to?

Many rules are not perfect, and it is often left to our 'common sense' as to when not to follow them.

Let's go back to our escorting visitors at all times rule. Imagine you are escorting a visitor, and there is nobody else in the vicinity. Your visitor starts to look unwell, and you suspect they are having a heart attack. The facility is electronically screened, and you cannot make a call for help. Your only option is to leave the person, and go and fetch help. Would you do this?

The visitor's life may be in the balance – every minute counts during a heart attack.

In this situation, most people would consider an unwritten rule – that saving a person's life is more important than following the organisation's security guidelines.

This takes us back to me, as an inspector. Does this make me a visitor? Remember, I told the employees that I had a legal right of entry. They were following my instructions. Does this mean my instructions take priority over the company rules? In this case, when left alone in the secure area, it was indeed the case that my newly introduced rules and inspection procedure did take precedence.

When you consider that many rules are not very well thought out, and need interpretation by their users, it does make sense that, in the right circumstances, people disobey rules. In fact, having a culture that sticks too closely to rules can be a bad thing, as flexibility and creativity are lost. Cultural differences are seldom taken into account when developing global information security policies and procedures. As we saw in our hacking the cloud adventure, the social engineer exploits this.

This is a good example of one of two strategies that I have deployed, very much dependent upon the local culture that I expect to see. Recently, I presented on this very issue at Infosecurity Europe. I used two countries, Norway and India, as examples of opposite ends of a continuum with regard to compliance with rules. Of course, this is quite a generalisation, but as we have already discussed, these sorts of generalisations can be useful. The acid test is always: does it work in making your social engineering easier? If so, then it is a valid technique – a real attacker will not take the moral high ground.

The reason I selected Norway and India was because I had some recent social engineering experience that I could refer to directly. In my experience, the cultural differences with regard to following instructions were very different. In the case of Norway, it is quite usual for people to directly challenge instructions from their boss. In contrast, India still retains very strong social hierarchies – people tend to follow instructions, without question, if the right person gives the instruction.

These cultural tendencies each have associated social engineering vulnerabilities:

Norway – although they are very likely to challenge the authority figure, they are equally willing to deviate from established procedures if they are given sufficient (and logical) reason for doing so.

India – whilst adherence to strict procedures is generally very good, if you can establish that your authority is greater than that of the established procedure, then they are very likely to follow your instructions.

Therefore, as a social engineer, you simple adapt your techniques according to the local culture.

It is worth noting that these generalisations apply less as we have an increasing flow of people across boundaries, either for education or employment. With increasing globalisation, this trend will no doubt continue.

For this adventure, you might say that my choice of pretext and identity helped a great deal, and you would be correct. This is a feature of social engineering – smart planning and good preparation brings you luck. Of course, you still have to play the part and be convincing, and also think on your feet.

People often ask me how I manage to play these roles, and in particular, if it requires any acting training. In my case, I take the 'method acting' route – that is, to believe in the role.

In this adventure, for most of the time I really 'believed' I was an inspector. The more you believe what you are saying, the more naturally you will behave, and aspects such as body language will automatically follow – and be realistic to your target.

Pre-Warned Security Guards

I recently conducted a variation on this attack, with a colleague playing the role of the inspector, while I was an employee showing him around a number of satellite offices for a multinational company. These offices were quite close to a main office, so we could efficiently test each of them in a single day.

The scenario was simple: I would turn up with what looked like an employee ID, and the inspector had some visitor ID that looked as if he was already signed in at the main office. Of course, both IDs were fake.

Mine was meant to operate the swipe system at the main office, but not at each satellite. Therefore, the security guards would have to sign us in.

This was quite a simple test, designed to check that the guards would follow processes.

You might think that a security guard would be expected to allow someone who obviously looked like an employee to enter. However, there was an established process that employee credentials should be checked on the centralised access system. Therefore, to give the security guards a fighting chance, I used my own name on my ID, so that the guards could catch us out just by following the 'normal' process.

Of course, I was also interested in what they would do if they didn't find me on the system. This might take a few courses of action:

1. They might interpret this as a system fault, and let me in. This has happened before on a number of occasions. If we look, and act, in a 'trustworthy' manner, then the security guard may decide that a system fault is the most likely answer to not finding me on the system.

2. They might be confused, and allow me to provide the answer. I planned to use the excuse that I was new, and therefore might not be on the system. If you confuse someone's mental processes, then they become very open to persuasion. You just wait for the look of confusion and internal debate on their face, and then provide a convenient solution – and instruction on how they should react.

If the guard didn't give us instant access, I would expect to observe the security guard going through some distinct mental processes as he tried to make sense of the situation.

On a superficial level, the security guard did all the right things:

Firstly, he checked my ID on the system. Having not found it, he phoned his boss, saying he needed to verify the visit. Then, having been told something, he asked to see my badge. Discovering that it was not a true pass, but a paper copy, we showed him a letter explaining this was a test.

However, this first office gave me a strange feeling in my gut. The guard was all wrong. What was it? He had done all the right things.

The answer was exactly that – it was too good, and he wasn't confused enough by the situation. In my extensive experience, people tend to go through the same observable processes, and this takes time. As the observer, I am focused on their reaction (although I act as if I am a little bored of waiting, and expecting them to give me access).

Did my colleague give the game away? I wasn't requiring much of him in this situation. It isn't difficult to look like a visitor.

Simple conclusion? The guard was expecting the test!

This happens, as a testing exercise proceeds, there is a risk that word gets around, even if everyone involved is sworn to secrecy. In this case, the speed at which he had phoned his boss was strange.

We had already embarrassed the facilities management team by breaking into the main office using pretty much the same scenarios as we had in a previous test. We had been commissioned by the information security team to carry out a range of tests – some new, and some to retest previous exploits.

Although 'improvements' had been made, it is difficult to maintain these, especially if team members change – as is often the case with physical security guards, where staff turnover can be quite high.

As we made our way to the next office, I started to analyse the situation at the first office, and why I was so convinced that he was expecting the test:

Why not ask who I was working with at the main office? If you cannot verify who someone is, then the next logical step is to verify the person they work for. He never gave me that chance. He was just too eager to phone his boss. It strongly suggested that he had been warned, and instructed to phone his boss if he spotted anything suspicious. However, it was this very behaviour that made his own actions suspicious to us.

Also, the guard wasn't surprised enough. Targets that uncover a test typically go through a range of emotions. They can be confused by the situation, slightly aggressive as they first challenge someone.

His first reaction was too controlled and immediate – he did not go through any deliberations. It was as if he was carrying out a recently issued instruction.

His visible emotions were a combination of relief and satisfaction at catching us. He also wasn't very surprised at this being a test – it was just confirming what he was looking for in the first place.

The more I examined the flow of actions, the more it became clear that the facilities manager had warned the guards at the remote sites. He was expecting a test.

The facilities manager had not known about the testing, but had been informed that morning, following some alerts been generated during the 'successful' testing at the main office. It is understandable that having found out that his security had already been breached twice that morning, he would not want to be further embarrassed by the afternoon testing. This was especially the case as the morning's exploits were a repeat test, using very similar methods and attack vectors.

So, what did this do to the remaining testing of the satellite offices?

The actions of other guards confirmed our initial suspicions:

- One guard that blocked our access phoned his boss immediately when we introduced ourselves. This time without any checks on the system. He identified me as not being an employee without actually checking.

- One guard looked very worried as soon as we walked in. He was distinctly sweaty, and clearly agitated. His relief at discovering this was the test was quite dramatic. He was clearly worried for his job.

However, you might be surprised to find out that we did, even though they were clearly expecting a test, still manage to gain entry into half of the satellite offices.

Why is this the case?

Well, even though the security guards had been warned to expect a test, they still didn't interpret our actions as being that test. This wasn't a great demonstration of their abilities, and did show how our scenario design was quite convincing.

There were additional clues within the guards that still gave us access that they were on the look out for something suspicious:

- One guard kept looking very suspiciously at us as he gave us access. You could see him thinking, "Is this the test I've been told about?" It was as if he was searching for a clue that this might be the test, but didn't want to challenge us without being sure. This is an indication that some people, even when faced with an actual intrusion, are still reluctant to believe that it might be malicious.

- Another guard left his desk to meet us at the door, which was very unusual, as I cannot believe that he did that each day for every visitor. That said, he still gave us access, having not interpreted our pretext as false.

Clearly, there was still going to be a chance that our visit was genuine, so the security guards had a dilemma: did they challenge everyone, ensuring they did identify the test, whilst running the risk of annoying someone?

In my experience, security guards are quite sensitive to being accused of stopping, or delaying, legitimate activities. Senior managers are often to blame here, as they frequently expect process to be bypassed to make their lives a little easier. Clearly, as a social engineer, I exploit this tendency.

The variation in processes between each guard was also interesting. If they had followed the 'normal' checking process, then we would have been discovered. However, the fact that they were expecting something unusual meant that they each responded differently to the increased stress of the situation. I suspect they had been told to, "Look out for the test, and contact me", by their boss – a variation in process, and therefore relatively easy for us to spot.

I wouldn't expect the facilities manager to own up to giving this warning, and sure enough, he didn't. I accepted that it might not have been him – the guards might have warned each other, and you cannot be 100% sure in these situations. However, the speed with which they phoned their boss indicated that the warning had come from him. If the guards had just 'spread the word', then I would have expected variation in their responses when they thought they had spotted the test. The call to their boss was just too quick, and his response too quick to be anything other than well rehearsed in his own mind.

It's interesting that even if typical security guards know a test is imminent, they can still be fooled.

Our scenario wasn't too difficult to see through. My use of a non-existent employee was designed to give the security guards a clue, and an opportunity to spot the test.

However, to be fair on the guards that still let us in, my fake employee badge was quite well executed, especially as it was constructed from memory and notes, and not from a photograph of a genuine badge.

Stealing The Crown Jewels

Introduction

I don't actually mean the real crown jewels – as in the Queen's bling that you can view in the Tower of London. I must apologise if you are offended by my irreverence to Her Royal Highness. I must confess to, having given this some thought, decided that I am a republican, and therefore against the concept of a 'royal' family.

I do have some respect for the current Queen Elizabeth II. She has 'served' her country tirelessly, and brought a level of respectability missing from many of the UK's previous monarchs. I also recognise that the British royal family do attract considerable tourism to the UK.

However, on balance, I am still a republican. Why? Because of the psychological effect on the nation, particularly on young people. At an early age, children learn about these 'special' people, and this gives the message that some people are destined for great things, with the corollary that you might not be. My vote would be for a meritocracy, with the associated positive messages about reward for hard work outweighing the tourist gains from the monarchy.

Anyway, back to the crown jewels. Much as it would interest me to be given this challenge, I would in all likelihood be prevented from writing about it if I did. What I refer to in the context of this challenge is that each organisation has its own most valuable information, its very own 'crown jewels'.

In this case, we are talking about a global company with many tens of thousands of employees across many countries. However, within this large global community, there exists a single document that has a particular value. For our purposes (and in order not to be too specific), I am going to call it the strategic plan.

This document is only ever seen by a maximum of about 30 people, and copies (both electronic and paper) are restricted accordingly. It is the most important document the board use. It contains key operational information, strategic analysis, and key information regarding the direction of the company, and it is constantly under review and regularly updated. Therefore, it gives up-to-the-minute information on the direction of the organisation and the board's strategic thinking.

The client is also operating in a very competitive and fast evolving environment. You can see why the 'crown jewels' label fits this document.

Also, there is another factor driving the clients' interest in our targeting this document – they knew that their main competitor had a previous copy. Their own 'insider' information from a key competitor had revealed this fact, although they did not have any intelligence as to how it had been acquired. Their own investigations had not revealed how this breach had been carried out.

The management response to the breach was to bring in ECSC to see how it could be done. At the very least, even if our techniques were not the same, it would result in more understanding of the human-related vulnerabilities, and therefore a chance to prevent future breaches.

This adventure is a great one to close the first part of *Hacking the Human II*:

1. The client brief was quite challenging, due to their organisational expertise in security and the very narrow target.

2. The site presented some serious physical access challenges.

3. The attack vectors brought together a number of elements of social engineering. This allows me to illustrate for you a relatively involved, multifaceted, exercise that uses a number of techniques (some of which you have already read about in our previous adventures).

The Challenge

The simple brief was to steal the strategic plan.

We had only sketchy information about the site, based on a single previous, quite brief, visit. However, it was enough to see that some extensive security was in place, including:

1. A manned site barrier for vehicles and pedestrians.

2. A barrier entry system from reception into the offices, with no security guards to let you through.

3. A professional information security team, with extensive staff awareness activities in place.

Thinking and Planning

My colleague Lucy joined me for this exercise. I have worked with Lucy for many years – long enough for her to know how I think (sometimes too much so). She makes a near-perfect social engineer, as she is very bright, and lightning quick at decision-making and thinking on her feet. In addition, she is extremely personable, with an ability to develop effective relationships very quickly. One day, she will lead her own company, and surpass my achievements with ECSC.

Lucy is also a valuable contributor to both the original *Hacking the Human* and this second set of adventures. She reviews every word that I write; telling me what will enhance my ideas, and what to remove (including the paragraph above – the only occasion where I ignored her instruction).

Anyway, back to the adventure. Lucy and I booked into a local hotel, where we could walk to the client site, and started to conduct some surveillance. Knowing the level of challenge, we made sure we had allocated enough resource to this.

Lucy managed to persuade (remember she is good at this) the hotel to give me a suite for the price of a standard room, so we had a good base from which to develop our plan of attack.

The whole site was surrounded by a high fence, with extensive CCTV coverage. Although I did find some blind spots, exploiting them would involves either breaking the fence or climbing across it – neither of which really fit with our brief of exploiting human weaknesses.

I also found a way under the fence, in a CCTV blind spot. However,

Lucy doesn't like getting dirty, and only had heels with her in the shoe department. Therefore, we had to find a people-related vulnerability.

We often concentrate some surveillance activities on the start and end of the working day. This allows us to observe processes that might not have been evident during my previous visit.

Lucy spotted it first – a bus. This was clearly dedicated to employees, as it was allowed through the site barriers and had about 20 people disembark. Also, and most critically, they went into the facility through a rear entrance, rather than via the front of the building.

Although from our external surveillance point, we couldn't directly see the layout of this rear entrance, we had strong suspicions that it would not have a swipe barrier system:

1. Barrier systems are quite expensive.

2. The entrance didn't seem to be in use during the rest of the day, and therefore might not warrant such expenditure.

We managed to get to my car quickly enough to follow the bus, and ascertained that it was a free service from the city centre.

This looked like our potential first vulnerability.

We continued with our planning, and prepared for a number of scenarios that could help us once on site. In our experience, you need a range of planned approaches, and also to be prepared to ditch all the planning at an instants notice if you spot either an unexpected threat, or more importantly, a new opportunity. This must be one of the most fun jobs going!

Attack Strategy

Lucy followed her observation regarding the free bus service and placed a call to reception, as an auditor due to start working for the company the following week, asking if we could use the free bus, and to get details of where it set off from.

Of course, they were helpful.

Having learned its starting point, the next morning we spent time near the pickup point and noticed a number of employees waiting, both near the bus stop and in the nearest coffee shop. A number of people were wearing their company ID badges whilst waiting for the bus, and Lucy managed to covertly photograph one of the badges with her iPhone.

I used a slightly different approach, as I usually do, and simply sketched the details of the badge through observing a few different people. This is common practice for me – often within five minutes of sitting in a reception area, I have enough notes to duplicate the full range of employee, contractor and visitor badges present.

My notes aren't sufficient to create a perfect copy. However, if I replicate what I see from a short distance, the results are always good enough to satisfy the glancing observation of a receptionist or security guard. My target's view is likely to be similar to mine when making notes on the copy.

We had equipped the hotel suite as an effective base of operations – one capable of facilitating our new badge forgery task. Yes, we did remember to keep the 'do not disturb' sign in place when we weren't there, so that our activities were not inadvertently discovered by hotel staff.

Armed with our newly made employee badges, Lucy and I joined the free bus. The driver made no attempt to check badges at that point.

As planned, the bus took us through the barriers to enter the site and towards the rear of the building.

As we departed the bus, we could clearly see the rear entrance, with a security guard. He appeared to have two roles: firstly, he was checking badges, and secondly, making sure that everyone swiped their access card when entering. This was necessary, as the door had no barriers.

Unfortunately, he had made a simple error, in that he had located himself well within the building, and therefore couldn't actually check that everyone had swiped.

Personality Profile

The security guard looked quite typical: middle-aged man, stocky
build. Perhaps an ex-police officer topping up his pension? Probably
not, on reflection: this used to be common, but with security guards
earning so little and police pensions being relatively generous, I
find this less and less.

He looked reasonably engaged, if in the wrong position to make
sure that people actually swiped to get in.

I would place him as being more Amiable than Analytical, so
not much of a barrier.

You might think I am a bit harsh on security guards. However,
this is my experience – they present little challenge.

I do, however, come across some notable exceptions.

In one organisation, I had tricked my way into a rear entrance,
having made my way around the back of the organisation on foot.
I was making my way up a stairwell when the senior security guard
suddenly appeared and challenged me.

He was not the usual personality profile – really a combination
between Driver and Analytical (a powerful combination for such a
role).

I asked him what brought me to his attention.

"It was a bit of luck, really – I was watching the CCTV and saw
you moving around the back – you just looked wrong."
Wow – great explanation. This was an experienced individual
listening to their subconscious.

I don't tend to 'look wrong', so he did well, especially over
CCTV. It was very commendable.

I fed back to the client that this individual was exceptional and

> should be retained at all cost. They informed me that he was leaving
> shortly to head up security for a much larger organisation. It was
> someone else's gain and this company's significant loss.

Back to our less impressive guarding of the rear entrance.

We simply joined the small queue (having positioned ourselves in the
middle of the bus, to keep us in the middle of the departing employees).
We could then offer our badges to the reader – which of course, didn't
beep. However, the door was open from the previous person, so we could
enter.

We then showed our ID cards to the guard, without being too obvious
about it, and gained entry.

This was the first hurdle accomplished – we were now on site.

We did later leave the site, and then return a number of times,
demonstrating a number of weaknesses to the external security, including:

1. We entered the site on foot. We did this at lunchtime, carrying
    bags from the local fast-food takeaway, demonstrating the relaxed
    checks on anyone arriving by foot.

2. I drove onto the site, having photographed (and recreated) a staff
    pass that people had in the windscreens (not much more than a
    coloured piece of paper).

3. Lucy entered through another rear door at the end of the day, taking
    the opportunity to come in as someone was leaving.

4. I came through to reception, in the middle of a mobile phone
    conversation, loitering   long enough to tailgate through a side
    entrance that connected reception to the main office without going
    through the main swipe entry and barrier system.

This gave us enough routes of entry to clearly demonstrate a range of
weaknesses, and show that the risk of someone gaining access to the
site was realistic. It was our intention to 'get caught' in at least one of

these attempts, to satisfy our methodology of measuring the effectiveness of controls through a mixture of results. However, we are not always successful in getting caught.

Now it was time to gain access to the crown jewels – the strategic plan.

This presented two challenges:

Firstly, we didn't know who had access to the key document.

Secondly, we didn't know where it would be stored.

We decided on a two-pronged attack strategy: Lucy would obtain passwords, whilst I gained details of the plan, who had access and where it was located.

Lucy did a combination of remote phishing (along the lines of our previous adventure), combined with some local 'auditing' – again, similar to my approach described previously. She was busy collecting logins – and making friends as she stole from them.

I decided to head to the executive suite, and see who had the plan.

Execution & Techniques

Being a personal assistant (PA) can be quite lonely. You tend to work in relative isolation, alongside your particular executive, and you can miss out on the normal interaction with a number of people. Often your role is to protect the executive from unwanted visitors and calls. However, PAs are useful for the social engineer, as they often have the access rights of their boss.

"Hello, I'm Ian. Can I sit with you for a few minutes?" I might have said "bother" or "interrupt", rather than "sit" – these are perhaps more natural introductions, but also have more negative consequences and might lead to an initial annoyance.

I selected a PA attached to a large (empty) executive office. I wanted someone who had an important boss, and where the boss wasn't present. I assumed they would have some time on their hands (relative to when the boss was on site), and would welcome a chat with a nice auditor.

Personality Profile

This lady had quite a stern look initially; very Analytical, with some Driver in her speed of reaction to my communication – certainly far to the right in the personality matrix.

This is partly expected from someone who interacts with senior managers, and is expected to act in the role of gatekeeper for her boss.

Psychological Techniques

As she was an Analytical personality, it was important that I gave her lots of information for her to fully understand the situation. If you present a detailed and logical argument for your actions, you get compliance.

This can be combined with being friendly. Analyticals can find human relationships challenging, and therefore respond well to finding a 'genuine' friend.

People do find it difficult to distinguish between genuine friends and those who are simply manipulating them. That is why the traditional con artist has been so successful, and why diplomats continually fall for very predictable amorous approaches from someone much too young and good looking to be a realistic catch for them.

We are programmed to be drawn to friendship, particularly if it is accompanied with signs of attraction from the other party.

"I'm doing some auditing of information security, and have been asked to look at security around executive information."

I started having a nice conversation with my target. We actually talked less about security, and more about the organisation, the CEO (whom she looked after), and her family.

People like to talk – and more importantly, they love to be listened to. It is a worthwhile investment in your social engineering to develop a relationship with some good active listening.

I explained that I was particularly interested in how they protected the most confidential documents, and where these were stored. This was important, I said, as my colleague was checking the access rights of a number of folders within the network shared drive. I explained that the main focus of the audit was IT security.

She showed me the work she did, preparing board papers and handling a variety of communication for a number of executives. But there was no mention of the strategic plan.

"I am aware that the strategic plan is a good example of a very confidential document," I said. "Do you ever handle it?"

"No, I've never seen a copy. The CEO keeps it in his safe."

So now I had a challenge. It is normally safe to assume that all executive documents go through the PAs. In this case, I would need to target the CEO directly.

I am not a professional safe-cracker. I would only describe myself as a gifted amateur. I do find the area of lock-picking to be quite interesting. By that, I mean real manual lock picking, not just using a bump key or similar automated lock-picking tool (these are now so commonly available that the challenge isn't interesting anymore).

Anyway, that sort of activity is really beyond our brief to exploit human vulnerabilities, so I had to come up with a different strategy.

Now, as it happens this was a case in point where an opportunity (some might call it luck – but you know what I think about 'luck') came my way:

"The best people to help you with that would be the business intelligence team, as they produce the plan. Would you like me to introduce you?"

I didn't need to think for too long about my reply, although I did make sure I didn't show my enthusiasm too much:

"Yes, that would be fine. Thank you."

Notice that I didn't say "fantastic", or "excellent". You need to keep your reactions quite low key when you hit gold, and not give away any excitement you might be feeling.

My new best friend walked me down the corridor and knocked on a locked door. I heard a key turn, and a face appeared around the door.

"Hello Jim, this is Ian, he needs to ask you some questions about the strategic plan."

Now, even if you were to work in an office so secure that you had to lock it with a key even when you were inside, you would still likely comply with a request from the CEO's PA.

Sure enough, Jim invited me in with a: "What do you need to know?"

Personality Profile

Jim was what you might expect of someone with his head in complex business data: very Analytical. However, I wanted to explore what direction from Analytical he tended to lean, as this can be key to my attack approach.

In this case, he appeared to have Expressive tendencies, placing him on an interesting diagonal axis between the two.

I could tell this partly by the way he dressed, but also his tendency to talk about "looking good".

Psychological Techniques

So, as an Analytical, you might give him lots of information, and be his friend. However, the Expressive tendencies meant that he needed a quicker pace of communication to feel comfortable.

I talked to Jim for a while, learning about the process of creating the plan, keeping it up to date and communicating it (securely) to the executives.

I explained that I was investigating security, and in particular, how the

IT department secured critical network folders. It would be helpful if he showed me which locations he used to store the strategic plan. Jim, by now also my best friend, duly obliged.

I wasn't sure if Lucy was having much success with her password harvesting (although I shouldn't have doubted her abilities), so I took the opportunity to try the (by now old) "I have been told to trick you into telling me your password" routine. As previously explained, this involved getting Jim to type his password into my laptop. He fell for this one.

I now had not only the location of the plan, but also a working login and password which to access it.

Unfortunately, the client used two-factor remote access, so armed only with a username and password, we would have to use an internal computer to access the plan.

Lucy and I met up for a break, and left the site with the intention of returning later armed with our collection of logins (she had many, and I had Jim's).

Arriving at 7 p.m., we split up, finished our site entry testing (described above), and met up at an agreed internal location to put our new logins to good use.

We picked a quiet corridor, with the lights already turned off, and located ourselves in an office where we could work without being visible from the corridor. We could then try a number of logins, and demonstrate access to a range of confidential documents. Lucy had obtained not only the access credentials of her targets, but also the location of their most confidential documents.

Results & Analysis

We had the strategic plan. Actually, we had a photo of the front cover visible on screen, taken whilst conducting our evening username and password exploration.

As previously discussed, we don't remove documents unless absolutely necessary. This is both because we don't want to risk losing them and because we don't need to steal them to demonstrate the effectiveness of our exploitation of vulnerabilities.

Clearly, this client had physical security weaknesses that were not immediately apparent due to their security site perimeter and barriers – both for vehicles and pedestrian entry.

In addition, as is often the case, this perceived secure perimeter led to a level of internal trust when we approached people at their desks.

In principle, the security around the strategic plan looked very good. Documents were kept in private safes, and not even shared with PAs. However, someone has to create these, and using a 'normal' network login meant that they were vulnerable to a range of attacks.

We actually found a number of Lucy's username and password combinations also gave us access to the plan. This was because she had decided to target the IT department. Her thinking was that I might not gain access directly through my chosen route, so she had better obtain some accounts with administration level access. Sure enough, a number of the accounts she compromised did have full access to the whole shared drive, including the location of the strategic plan.

Our feedback to the board was quite interesting.

Personality Profile

Our final personality encountered during these Part One adventures was an extreme Driver (tightly placed in the top left corner of the personality matrix). This was unexpected from the chairman of a multinational company, as you don't reach these heights ambling along with the Amiables, or too tied up in detail with the Analyticals.

One interesting aspect of the extreme Driver is the speed of their conscious thought processes – it's as if they have a turbo charge feature. Once engaged on a topic, they speed ahead, usually overtaking the communicator of the information that they are absorbing. You will probably recognise this behaviour in at least one of your bosses.

I had been warned by the information security manager that the chairman had a tendency to start up conversations with the executive next to him during presentations. I just took this to be because all presentations were too slow for him.

The chairman had a great stare – very direct and almost penetrating. You find this with extreme Drivers. The usual rules about looking up to access visual memories don't appear to apply – everything is in direct focus in front of them. As they access memories, you will see them adjust their focus – they are placing their visual memories directly over their field of vision. This is why you might feel that they are disengaged – it's because they are.

You cannot keep up with the processing speed of a brain like this. The best you can hope is to keep stimulating it to keep its interest.

Psychological Techniques

If I were just communicating to the chairman, I would have adjusted up to his speed. I sometimes even miss out words and chunks of sentences – adding to the speed. They don't notice. You can push the key information at them faster and faster, and they love it.

You need to listen carefully, adapt your language to visual concepts, and keep up.

I often interact with IT specialists, as they frequently end up in information security management roles. People still think information security is the same as IT security, and therefore gravitate to technical specialists. This is partly why the human aspect of security gets neglected.

I have recently been working with one of these people, who is clearly very analytical. One of his challenges is that senior management are not fully engaged (to say the least). Therefore, a strategy I have been working with him on is to present key information in simple pictures (graphs and trends). And I constantly tell him not to include too much information.

Analyticals tend to believe that senior managers cannot understand situations, and therefore make the correct decisions, without giving them 'all the information they need'. This is the level of information that the Analytical needs. Of course, the Driver personality quickly gets bored with this – and then turns their attention elsewhere.

A better strategy with Drivers is to get straight to the heart of the problem: show it to them in a picture. Be ready with the detail to back it up, but don't be offended if you don't have to use it. Once you have the trust of a senior manager, and they know that you have done the analysis, why do they need to waste their time repeating this work themselves?

Then be ready with options for solutions, as they will want this immediately. If you don't give them thought out options, they will make up their own on the spot – and these might not be as good as yours.

I actually find senior managers some of the easiest people to get onside with an issue. This is because they find taking decisions easy - they do a lot of it. Therefore, presented with the right information in the way they understand it, they reach the 'right' decision.

Anyway, back to my super-Driver chairman.

With a full board of directors in the room, I had to play to the whole audience – although I was relying on a good proportion of them being Driver personalities. So my presentation went straight to the point.

"We were commissioned to steal your strategic plan, using social engineering techniques. We succeeded after only XX days of effort."

Our presentation slide showed the front cover of the strategic plan visible on a computer screen.

> That got their attention.
>
> "Now, let me show you how we did it."
>
> Sure enough, within the first couple of minutes, the chairman started to whisper to his colleague. However, I could tell they were commenting on the content – they were clearly referring to it (pointing is a giveaway).

At first, the chairman was a little dismissive, saying that he thought we were probably much more talented than any thief, and that the whole scenario of stealing the strategic plan was unrealistic.

The chairman's view evolved over the course of the meeting, particularly when he heard:

1. That their competitor had previously obtained a copy – something of which he was not aware.

2. The chief operations officer explaining that he used to conduct similar reconnaissance against their competitors in his younger days.

The chairman's change of heart was further demonstrated a few months later, when he addressed the company with key strategic targets for the next year – and information security was one of them.

This is quite typical of the amount of movement you get when communicating effectively with senior managers.

I find many middle and junior managers complain about senior managers "not listening" and not coming to decisions quickly enough.

I actually find the complete opposite. The vast majority of senior managers are very quick at making decisions. They just need their options presented to them in a way that they can quickly understand. In general, they are the easiest of all personalities to obtain quick decisions from.

If you have difficulty communicating with your managers, and getting them to make decisions in line with your arguments, then you clearly need a better understanding of the way people think and how they reach decisions. And that leads us perfectly into Part Two.

PART TWO
The New Subconscious

Introducing Your Brain

As a consultant, averaging 15 nights a month in hotels, I often eat alone. Tonight was no different. So, armed with my notebook and pen (yes, I am still quite traditional in this respect), I began to map out Part Two of *Hacking the Human II*. I already had plenty of notes and ideas, so this evening was about bringing some structure and flow – adding a logical process. I like to think that I displayed creativity and logic; adding connections and inventing suitable headings for each chapter. My brain processes (no doubt helped by a rather fine king prawn biryani) displayed the range of skills that make humans unique on this planet.

However, in my travels as a social engineer, I also come across many instances of people doing silly things that help my team and I bypass information security. These are not people who lack intelligence. In fact, I see very little correlation between intelligence and poor decision-making that can be exposed by the social engineer. Actually, there has been some research that suggests people who come under the control of religious cults are actually more likely to be highly educated. It can be argued that the effects of a cult are similar to the attacks by a social engineer – taking someone down a path of action that can be against strict logic, often by instilling alternative beliefs.

As a social engineer, the study of decision-making is central, as each human vulnerability is related to a decision that an individual makes, either to bypass a security control, or perform an action that hasn't been anticipated or planned for.

In order to understand the way that behaviour, and decision-making, affects security, I widen my observations to all aspects of our actions. I am particularly interested in behaviour that isn't logical. By way of everyday examples, why do people:

1. Eat too much, despite knowing that it is having a negative effect on their health?

2. Smoke, even when they know it will shorten their life by 10 years?

3. Consume an excess of alcohol, even after recognising the negative effects on their life and long-term health?

These are examples of where behaviour can conflict with logic. At one level, an individual wants to change their actions, but they fail to do so. It is as if they are not in control of their own body – so who, or what, is in control? Where are these decisions being made?

Looking at information security, professionals try to design a set of logical processes for your organisation, and then, as can be seen in Part One, using social engineering, my team and I make users bypass these security countermeasures.

In this second part of *Hacking the Human II*, I will explore with you the workings of your brain. You need to be warned that you might not like this. Aspects of our exploration might conflict with your current beliefs, and may at times make you feel uncomfortable.

It is my belief that your beliefs can be temporary. They can be treated as a conclusion to your current thought processes that may be subject to revision in the light of new evidence. A belief that is fixed and unwavering works against the development of you as an individual, our society, and the evolution of our species.

By including the word 'evolution' and 'species' in the previous paragraph, I intentionally placed a firm starting point to the foundations of my own (current) beliefs. This may be in stark contrast to beliefs you may (currently) hold. I simply ask you to try and be open-minded and consider the evidence as presented to you.

Actually, I prefer you don't 'try' to be open minded. People who 'try' often fail. Much better to just 'succeed' from the outset and sidestep the 'try' phase. Therefore, I simply ask you to be open-minded throughout Part Two of *Hacking the Human II*.

Then you can make up your own mind! Actually, I don't think that you, or anyone else, can - but more of that later. By the time you understand that you aren't actually in charge of your own mind, and your actions, it will be too late.

Let's start the exploratory journey with a critically important area of human activity:

I play a pretty mean electric guitar. When on form, my fingers become a blur, and I can (on a good day) articulate 18 notes per second.

You may be asking yourself why this is important, although I find it difficult to work out why everyone doesn't need this skill – in my opinion, it should be added to the national curriculum. Actually, you may also be asking why extreme guitar playing is so important to the exploration of the subconscious.

It is absolutely critical, because:

1. Most people can't do this, apologies if you can.

2. I also can't do it if I 'try' and, importantly, if I think about it too much.

Now, I am confident that our brains (and fingers) are likely to have pretty much equal capability. In fact, my study of other equally fast guitar players leads to the conclusion that I am not particularly advantaged physically (in the department of fast fingers). Others have a better size and shape of hand, and a greater 'fast twitch' muscle percentage.

Please excuse my assumption that you have not developed what I consider to be this essential life skill. My guess is that you have found more productive things to do with your life than develop this ability. Please also note that I am not claiming to be the fastest musician on the planet – just one of them.

I developed this ability through a combination of late teenage obsession, combined with time on my hands at university (a distinct lack of interest in study in my late teens also helped me in this regard).

Don't worry – with the appropriate guidance, and 10 hours a day of practice for a couple of years, you, too, could share this exceptional 'gift'.

Why is this an important start to our exploration of the subconscious? Quite simply, it is because I can't play that fast – well, not consciously. But I have effectively trained my subconscious to do it for me.

After university, I also taught other people how to play in this way, so had a great opportunity to test out ideas and see what achieved the best results for a wide range of individuals.

For you budding musicians, the secret to learning to play so fast is to practice slowly – *very* slowly. It's not particularly intuitive, but it works. It is only through repeated, slow and precise repetition (to help I use a metronome, a device that marks time at a selected rate) that you develop the 'muscle memory' necessary to play faster than you can (consciously) think.

The term 'muscle memory' is very interesting. Do we really think our muscles contain memory? They certainly develop the required strength, speed, and range of movement, but do we really think they remember how to move? Anatomical study shows us that specific muscle movements are controlled with nerve impulses from the brain. (To simplify things somewhat, I don't intend to distinguish between the brain and the spinal cord – for our purposes, let's just assume that they combine to perform the function of the brain).

In rationalising my ability to play guitar so fast, what do I actually 'think'? It depends on the circumstances.

However, broadly it fits into two categories, which I will at this stage refer to as:

1. Semi-conscious. Here I am giving a certain amount of direction. Perhaps I know the scale, or pattern I wish to use. Sometimes, I want to get from note A to B via a certain route. My conscious brain is 'in control', but not supplying every detail of each finger movement.

2. Unconscious. This tends to happen when playing live, or in the studio when you get into what musicians call 'the zone'. Here, you tend to consciously drift away from thinking specifically about notes you wish to play. This is a special place to be – you might call it being inspired. In some cases, you can be genuinely surprised at what you play.

The second scenario applies much more to musical improvisation. By the way, for electric guitarists, pulling funny faces is an unintended consequence of this second state of mind. The precise reasons for this are as yet not fully understood, as academics have not devoted that much time to the study of extreme electric guitar playing. Perhaps pulling funny faces gives you an inherent advantage in learning a musical instrument, or perhaps the playing of an instrument helps to cultivate this skill. However, I have observed that this phenomenon does appear to apply much more to electric guitar players than other musicians.

Whilst you might not (contrary to my expectations) be particularly interested in my electric guitar playing, you should be interested in conscious and subconscious processing, and most critically, decision-making.

You cannot think consciously about, and direct, the movements required to play 18 notes per second, so another part of the brain has to be involved. I will refer to this as the subconscious initially, although you will find psychologists give this different titles.

Many processes start with conscious control, but with 'practice', the subconscious learns what is required and takes over the process. This is commonly observed to be the development of a skill – where an activity that others perceive as difficult is made to look effortless.

You might hear psychologists refer to this state as 'flow', from Mihaly Csikszentmihalyi's *Flow: The Psychology or Optimal Experience* (Harper, 1990). It is a state of effortless control.

In *Hacking the Human*, I used the familiar example of driving a car. Those of you who have learned to drive will appreciate how tricky it is when new to you. Your conscious brain is struggling to cope with controlling multiple movements involving hands and feet, combined with concentrating on other road users.

As you progress, you reach an optimum skill level. This is where your subconscious takes over the mechanics of controlling the vehicle, with your conscious brain able to concentrate on your surroundings.

However, you can also then progress to a potentially more dangerous level where your subconscious also starts to take over the analysis of your surroundings. You will recognise when this happens – you will arrive at home (or work) and find it difficult to remember the last few miles (or kilometres). The reason it will be home or work is that it will happen for a familiar route – your subconscious has learned the route and begins to take over.

This is where you hear of people who perhaps hit a pedestrian and say they 'didn't see them'. They are telling the truth – actually, it was their subconscious that failed to take notice of this person, whilst their conscious brain was disengaged from the activity.

Therefore, I would like you, for the moment, to accept the 'belief' that the subconscious is capable of learning. It can take repeated actions and allow them to become automatic - not requiring direct control from your conscious brain. This process is a useful skill. It enables mastery of a given activity - and also frees your conscious brain to concentrate on something else that could be more important.

What are the origins of this? Well, simply think of the primeval human, engaged in the activity of gathering a particular food – an activity repeated many times a day. It is a definite survival advantage to be able to do this whilst focusing on other things, like keeping a look out for potential threats. It's also possible that the recognition of threat is the subconscious process, leaving you to consciously concentrate on the location of food (or even a mate).

However, the subconscious isn't just about taking over repeated tasks and freeing up the conscious brain for other more potentially important duties.

In *Hacking the Human*, I made the following (somewhat controversial) assertion:

"All decisions we take are taken by the subconscious."

I then went further, adding:

"If necessary, the conscious mind invents a 'logical' justification for the decision. In effect, the conscious brain is in a constant state of delusional belief that it is control."

Although many people find this concept somewhat uncomfortable, recent academic research is now starting to prove its validity.

One example is the catchily titled article "Deciding Advantageously Before Knowing the Advantageous Strategy" (*Science*, February 1997). Here, the researchers Bechara, H Damasio, Tranel, and A R Damasio explored the decision-making behind a relatively simple betting game.

Players were given $2,000, and asked to play a game that involved turning cards from four desks. Some cards gave a win and some a loss. Two decks were engineered to give an overall loss and the other two to give an overall win. The experiment was to see when the individual could tell the difference between the two.

An added twist was that the researchers were not just looking for a conscious recognition of the difference between the cards. They also measured a subconscious response. They measured skin conductance response (SCR), which is basically small changes to your sweat levels. In a state of heightened tension, you sweat more, so your skin conductivity changes. This is termed 'anticipatory' SCR.

Rather predictably, players who encountered losses began to generate SCRs and avoided the decks with the large losses.

What is particularly interesting is when SCR changes started – when the player behaviour changed, and when players consciously recognised their playing strategy had changed. As soon as 10 cards into the game, players started showing changes in SCR, linked to the choice of the decks linked to losses. However, nobody consciously acknowledged any clue as to the set-up of the game until at least card 20. It took most people until about card 50 before they consciously started to notice a difference.

The remarkable observation was that people were changing their playing behaviour (in favour of the advantageous decks) before they consciously acknowledged any recognition of the difference.

This experiment shows not only that the subconscious recognised the threat first, but also how it changed the decisions the players made.

Critically, the conscious brain had no idea that this process was happening. Or, as the authors, rather academically, put it, "The activation of covert biases preceded overt reasoning."

The authors also expressed their conclusion in the following:

"We suspect that the autonomic responses we detected are evidence for a complex process of nonconscious signalling, which reflects access to records of previous individual experience – specifically, of records shaped by reward, punishment, and the emotional state that attends them."

As you can imagine, proving something like subconscious control is difficult. Asking a human to understand how their own brain works is always going to be problematic - how do you remove the inbuilt biases, conditioning, personal belief systems, and inherent delusions?

However, for the purposes of social engineering, I am not always looking for absolute proof – only evidence that a concept works and is useful. New theories may evolve, and if they work better, then they will deserve to take the place of the subconscious control assertion. You should not interpret these findings, and my subsequent conclusions, as anything more than a current view that has proved useful in a social engineering context.

In the development of the first *Hacking the Human*, I drew mainly on my own background of using Neuro-linguistic Programming (NLP) and hypnosis techniques to develop a theoretical framework for the understanding of human vulnerabilities, as they relate to social engineering. For this follow-on book, I decided it was time to delve into academic research.

Previously, I had found the mainstream academic approach to psychology to be rather frustrating – lots of behaviours identified and labelled, but without any underlying framework of understanding. It seemed quite superficial.

However, I was aware of certain pieces of research that very much confirmed the overall theory from NLP and hypnosis in the role of the subconscious. As a result, I started to amass a tidy pile of academic reading, and began an interesting journey of discovery. Contrary to my previous understanding, an examination of the role of the subconscious actually goes back quite a long way within what you might call mainstream academic work.

Back in 1865, William Hamilton said:

"I do not hesitate to maintain, that what we are conscious of is constructed out of what we are not conscious of."

Just one year later E. S. Dallas said:

"Outside consciousness, there rolls a vast tide of life which is perhaps more important to us than the little isle of our thoughts which lies within our ken."

Other psychologies rejected the subconscious mind. Descartes famously said that the mind and body are separate, with the mind being just conscious processing.

Psychology owes a big debt to Freud, with his identification of the 'ego' (conscious) and 'id' (subconscious) in 1923, and later the 'super-ego'. His work on identifying subconscious processes was groundbreaking. However, because of some of his further theories of the underlying causes of behaviour, his approach led to something of a backlash within mainstream psychology. An alternative approach, focusing more on behaviour and less on internal mind processes, took hold. The 'behaviourists' ruled until the 1950s when experimental psychologists really started to explore the workings of the mind.

It was really in the 1970s that the power of the subconscious started to become more widely adopted by psychologists. It doesn't surprise me that people repeatedly find the concept that part of their hidden mind is controlling some (or all) of their actions to be challenging. Society is based on the concept that people are able to make rational decisions and are responsible (consciously) for their actions. This responsibility is learnt in childhood. You don't hear many children blaming their subconscious for their misbehaviour (if only they knew!)

Recognition of the subconscious (often referred to as the unconscious or nonconscious) is now becoming relatively mainstream. In fact, as I explored more recent findings, I found the notion that the subconscious mind does the vast majority of the work, and the conscious brain's belief in its control is somewhat illusionary, to be something suggested by a number of people in the field.

A leader in this field is the psychologist Daniel Wegner. His work *The Illusion of Conscious Will* is full of great examples to illustrate that we confuse correlation with causality. That is, we think about something, and mistake that thought as having caused an action. Wegner argues that the subconscious processing caused both the thought and the action.

Wegner and fellow psychologist Thalia Wheatley published an interesting paper in *American Psychologist* in 1999, titled "Apparent Mental Causation – Sources of the Experience of Will".

Their thinking was strongly influenced by the experiments of physiologist Benjamin Libet in 1983, where he showed that brain waves indicated that decisions were being made in advance of conscious recognition of that decision.

Libet showed that brainwaves indicated a decision had been taken 300 milliseconds before someone consciously recognised it. This may not seem to be a long time, but in the context of what might be a relatively short decision-making process, it's highly significant. The very fact that the researchers could spot the decision before the subject thought they had made it was groundbreaking.

In order to carry out their own test as to whether we invent the perception of free will connected with an action, Wegner and Wheatley constructed a neat experiment, where the participant would believe that they had performed an action when it actually was not under their control.

Participants were paired up, and each placed their fingers on what was in effect a large computer mouse. They were moving an object on a computer screen, and making it point at various items. The set up was reminiscent of a ouija board – where you cannot be sure who is in control of the movement of the object.

The participants were jointly controlling the 'mouse', and in turn, an object on the screen. They had to stop movement every 30 seconds or so. Then, each participant would rate on a scale of 0-100 whether they intended to make the object stop where it did indeed stop.

The participants had headphones on, and were hearing certain words that might correspond to items on the screen and also music as part of the experiment.

However, one of the participants was being tricked. Their partner was actually part of the experiment, and was receiving instructions as to what movements to carry out. The testers called the plant a 'confederate'.

Sometimes the confederate was instructed to control the movements, while at other times they were to allow the participant to take full control and just follow their 'lead'.

This allowed the researchers to accurately measure when the participant directed actions and when the confederate carried them out. They could then correlate this with the participants scoring of whether they had controlled the movement intentionally.

They found that the participant scored their intention to move more on whether they linked a suggestion of the target in their headphones, rather than on whether they actually caused the movement. So, if the evidence pointed to them being in control, then they believed it to be the case – even though the experiment could ensure that they had not been in control.

Wegner and Wheatley sum up our belief in our own conscious control as "believing that our conscious thoughts cause our actions is an error based on the illusory experience of will".

More recent research by J. D. Haynes in 2011, has shown that indications of a decision from brainwaves can be detected up to 10 seconds before you become consciously aware of the decision.

Wegner and Wheatley also suggest that the reason people feel that action under hypnosis is involuntary is that the condition of hypnosis switches off the link to the conscious – and the process of it inventing a rationale for its actions.

However, other psychologists have observed that following hypnosis, people are only too ready to invent a rationale for their actions. This is particularly the case where people are carrying out actions that have been planted in their subconscious during a period of hypnosis, after which, they readily invent a rationale for their behaviour.

The systematic study of hypnotism is somewhat inadequate, with different people competing to promote beliefs about what it actually is (or whether it even actually exists). As Wegner puts it in his excellent *The Illusion of Conscious Will*, "Discoveries and counter-discoveries abound in this field, making it impossible on reading the research literature not to get the feeling that every researcher in this area is studying something different."

Also, nobody appears to have actually studied what the hypnotist is doing – they all concentrate on the subjects of hypnosis.

There is no doubt that hypnosis can have some powerful effects. In particular, it allows control of the subconscious beyond the capability of the conscious mind. For example, studies have shown the ability of hypnotised subjects to control the pain associated with lengthy surgical and dental operations, without the use of any drugs.

Hypnosis also seems to be very powerful at getting people to forget memories, and then re-access them when instructed to, again under hypnosis.

The modern view is very much that Freud underestimated the role of the subconscious. I like the description from Timothy Wilson, who said in 2002 that rather than the conscious brain being the tip of the mental iceberg, it was more like "a snowball on top of that iceberg".

It makes sense that you are not aware of the bulk of your brain's processing. It has been estimated that our brains receive about 11 million pieces of information per second. Imagine being aware of all that processing. As we have evolved, and our senses have developed, it made sense for most of the processing to be done automatically, hidden to our conscious brains.

How much can you consciously think about?

When it comes to completing multiple tasks, it is generally accepted that more than three activities becomes somewhat of a challenge.

This working hypothesis – with the subconscious being in charge of the brain – has served me well. It underpins many approaches to social engineering techniques, and helps give you a framework to understand human security vulnerabilities. It also helps me design countermeasures to protect systems from human weaknesses – please refer back to *Hacking the Human* for more on this vital topic.

So, accepting that we have the concept of the brain being made up of two parts, the conscious and subconscious brains, exploring how to influence the subconscious and use its 'power' to direct actions is particularly fruitful in a social engineering context. I don't wish to repeat too much from *Hacking the Human*, but you really should explore NLP (the founders' writings from the mid 1970s are the most useful) and hypnosis (particularly hypnotherapy) techniques to sharpen your understanding in this area.

Why, then, do we need something new in this area? Simply because I am not yet satisfied. I am increasingly questioning the concept of the subconscious, particularly as a coherent single entity. We like to think of ourselves as a single human 'being'. Our brain is central to our identity, and therefore our natural tendency is to think in the singular. Having accepted the need for a subconscious, we tend to think in the singular for this, as well.

For the purposes of our exploration and analysis, I am making two (important) assumptions:

1. That you accept the concept of a subconscious element to your brain. I don't intend to try and persuade you on this matter. We have more important things to explore. There is a huge amount of eminent thinking in this area, and not really much to contradict this theory – other than a dogged belief that conscious thinking is all that there is.

2. We are discounting the effects, or presence, of what might otherwise be termed the 'soul'. This concept is better left to the history of ancient tribal beliefs and customs. Again, I see no need to offer proof (accepting that proving something doesn't exist is somewhat challenging, as the burden of proof lies with the believer). If you still hold onto some variation on these historic beliefs, then you may find elements of our exploration to be somewhat uncomfortable. However, my observation of religious believers shows that they have a seemingly endless ability to maintain their faith, despite the evidence, and have a near infinite capacity to see evidence to support their belief.

If you need a definition of the subconscious, then you might start with that given by Timothy Wilson:

"mental processes that are inaccessible to consciousness, but that influence judgments, feelings or behaviours."

As we shall explore in this second half of *Hacking the Human II*, the main question for the social engineer is the level of the influence in the above definition. I would like to replace 'influence' with 'dictates' – as we proceed, you can see to what extent you might agree with me.

If you have a leaning towards philosophy, rather than psychology, you might want to further your studies, looking into what philosophers have termed "conscious inessentialism" and "epiphenomenalism". (And people wonder why philosophy can be difficult for the layperson to understand)!

Because social engineering is about directing people into taking an action to facilitate an attack, an understanding of the processes that lead to decisions is going to be of central importance. As we delve further into the workings of the mind, and the role of the subconscious, I would like you to keep thinking about the implications of what this means for social engineering attacks.

Therefore, in order to progress our exploration of the mind, I ask you to accept that the subconscious exists. Now, let's start to explore how it affects our actions on a day-to-day basis.

The Great Divide

What is the intrinsic difference between humans and other species? Is it our conscious thought processes?

Our current dominance on this planet shows that we must have some very significant evolutionary advantage over our animal cousins. If we use a rather crude model – that we are like other animals, but just more evolved – then you might work on the assumption that the subconscious is common to all species, but the conscious brain is what sets humans apart.

This morning, I heard of some interesting new research into the thought processes of crows (yes, the birds). They had actually designed an experiment to test the crows against a selection of children.

The ability they were testing was related to the famous Aesop fable where a crow in desperate need of water drops pebbles into water to raise its level. This is actually a genuine ability that crows have been observed to have.

The experiment had a cunning twist: a number of vertical tubes where water was present, but out of the reach of the crows. The clever thing was that adding pebbles to the water had no effect – the experiment compensated for the pebbles by allowing water to drain away, maintaining the water at the same level. However, if the crow added pebbles to another tube (not containing water), the water in the original tube 'magically' rose.

Well, it turns out that the crows, which were able to raise water in a normal tube, could not learn this new magic set up. They were, in the words of the researcher, "absolutely useless". However, and this is the interesting bit, the (human) children learned the way to raise the level very quickly. They believed an effect that the crows could not accept.

This appears to show a learning ability in children not present in crows, which is not entirely, surprising really. If crows had an ability to learn over and above that of humans, then they would be in charge by now.

What was quite surprising was the researchers description of the children as having some "special" ability to accept illogical beliefs. I suggest that this observation is a mistake. They described this as an ability that is inherent in children. However, I believe that history is full of people of all ages taking on illogical beliefs as a way of interpreting and understanding their surroundings. This innate ability to accept events, and create beliefs, appears to be a human trait.

It appears to be the case that language (external and internal), particularly the language of logical argument, is what separates humans from other species. We have an ability to create an explanation for our observations - we create a logic. Unfortunately, this logic isn't necessarily correct.

Education and a scientific approach helps you build a more accurate model of your experience. Perhaps the researchers spend a little too much time with highly educated people with a very scientific (and conscious) approach to their decision-making.

However, we also appear to have the natural tendency to apply logic where there isn't any – a potentially dangerous trait.

Are You An Expert?

The subconscious is also key to the development of expertise. You might regard being an expert as a very conscious and logical process: you acquire knowledge and experience, and this translates into what we call expertise. However, the subconscious can also play a role here.

An example that psychologists often use is that described by Gary Klein in the book *Sources of Power* (MIT Press, 1999). This involves an experienced fire chief ordering his team out of a house fire. He reported doing this "without thinking". At a conscious level, he had little idea what was wrong; only that he sensed an unusual danger.

It was as if his subconscious had directed him to danger without conscious processing. It turns out his 'intuition' was accurate, as the floor he and his team had been on collapsed shortly after they had left.

Now, an isolated case such as this can be just a simple case of coincidence. How many times do firefighters act on similar feelings that turn out to give no indication of special danger? However, this case provides a good illustration of how expertise developed over time can lead to you developing an intuition of value.

In this case, the fire chief did report that the situation was unusual: it was very quiet, but also very hot. It turned out that the fire was actually below the firefighters in the basement of the property – hence the imminent floor collapse.

Intuition could be regarded as your subconscious communicating with you. So what makes this communication 'expert'? The key component here is experience, and a significant history of operating in a field and developing expertise. The subconscious is not very 'intelligent', in the way we would normally explain that term. However, it has the capacity to learn and communicate a level of recognition regarding a given situation to you based on that learning.

Therefore, if you are in a team of firefighters and the newly qualified firefighter gets a 'funny feeling' about a situation, you can (as much as is possible for firefighters), 'safely' ignore his input. However, if the most experienced person on the crew starts to issue warnings, based on his or her 'gut feeling', then you should take immediate notice.

The key measure as to the value of someone's intuition is the level of relevant experience they have related to the situation upon which they are commenting. There are times to ignore intuition, and times to listen to it. The skill is to know which route to choose. However, as we shall later see, decisions such as this are so directed by the subconscious that your conscious choice might turn out to be somewhat of an illusion after all.

The work of Gary Klein and his team is quite interesting. The area in which he specialises is termed 'naturalistic' decision making, as he studies the decisions that individuals make during their everyday activities.

This contrasts with most psychology investigations, as they often use students (usually psychology students). This somewhat limits the applicability of their research to 'everyday' situations. That is why I am always keen to make my observations during actual social engineering exercises, where the targets do not know they are being tested. This gives a rich source of data regarding the way that people react when they don't know they are in an experiment.

Another group that gets lots of attention with studying the workings of the brain is people who have suffered a mental impairment, either through an accident of some sort or being born with it. This can give interesting comparisons with 'normal' people. However, I think the applicability to everyday decision-making can be limited. It's a little bit like asking a doctor for health advice. Doctors aren't experts in health, as they are predominantly trained in illness.

For health advice, ask a healthy person - and model their beliefs and associated behaviours.

Another interesting feature in the study of naturalistic decision-making is that it often occurs where procedures are poorly defined. This gives an interesting parallel to social engineering – in an attack, we often try to create scenarios that the intended target does not expect, and to which, therefore, he or she does not have a pre-programmed response. In these cases, they have to make instant decisions – and we can guide them towards our intended outcome.

An observation that Klein made in studying a number of experienced firefighters, making decisions in stressful circumstances, is that they did not appear to evaluate a range of options. Rather, they tended to appear to make decisions very quickly and then justify the decision without evaluation. One firefighter even said, "I don't remember when I've ever made a decision."

Klein has termed these situations, where the first option is chosen by an experienced person,'recognition-primed' decision-making. It's a clear case of the subconscious supplying the answer to a problem.

This is similar to the concept of 'satisficing', picking the first option that works, without further evaluation, as originated by the sociologist and psychologist Herbert Simon in *Models of Man* (Wiley, 1957). Experts are great at this, whilst beginners need to evaluate lots of options. In a social engineering attack, we often force people who are not experts into this instant decision-making – which is why our direction of the subconscious helps get the outcome we require. Because experts in social engineering are very rare, it is no surprise that we don't tend to get responses to our testing that demonstrate expertise in repelling an attack.

It is also interesting to look at the way that individuals, with particular expertise, explain their ability to recognise situations. Klein describes firefighters who develop a belief that they have extra-sensory perception (ESP).

This applies to the firefighter above, who recognised subconsciously that there was imminent danger. His belief in ESP came from his analysis that he had no suspicion that the house had a basement, and that a fire could be beneath his team. However, he did recognise that something wasn't right – particularly that the room was too hot for the size of observable fire. In this case, his subconscious decided, and the conscious justification was that ESP told the firefighter of the danger.

There are times when asking an expert to perform analysis can actually lead to worse decisions, as described by Wilson and Schooler in their 1991 article "Thinking too much: introspection can reduce the quality of preferences and decisions".

Another example, also studied by Klein and also where the person involved had a belief that he must have ESP, was that of Michael Riley.

Riley was an anti-air warfare specialist aboard the Royal Navy ship HMS Gloucester in the first Gulf War in 1992. Riley had an immensely difficult task – spotting missiles heading for ships in the Gulf. The difficulty was in distinguishing these missiles from 'friendly' aircraft. Clearly, mistakes have significant consequences: missing a missile means a ship being hit; wrongly identifying a missile means attacking a plane from your own side. Both outcomes mean that your colleagues are likely to be killed.

The challenge for Riley and his team was that the missiles they were looking out for closely resembled American A-6 aircraft returning from their bombing runs. The two are similar size, travel at the same speed, and have the same radar profile.

Riley's task was made more difficult by the fact that American pilots had been flying across suspected Silkworm missile sites on their return (even though they had been told not to), and had a habit of not activating their Identity Friend or Foe (IFF) system when leaving the coast.

The only (reasonably) reliable way to tell the difference was through altitude, but the *Gloucester* didn't have any altitude-capable radar.

At 5 o'clock one morning, Riley spotted a target leaving the coast of the Gulf. HMS *Gloucester* was only 20 miles off the coast (part of the force protecting the USS *Missouri*). Riley made a 'decision' in 40 seconds, and shot down the target. Riley said he 'knew' the target was a missile within five seconds of it appearing (this is after only two radar sweeps). The objective evidence didn't appear to give any indication to justify his apparently very strong belief in his decision. He was right, and he probably saved many lives with this decision.

You might come to a logical conclusion that this was just luck – after all, there have been many cases of the military shooting down their own aircraft (and even civilian airliners that haven't deviated from commercial flight paths), having been convinced that they were looking at an attacking plane or missile. However, investigators did uncover something that might have given Riley a subconscious indication of the threat.

Although the radar he was using did not give altitude information, the altitude of a target could be inferred by how far from the coast a target first appears on the radar. A low altitude target would be further from the coast, so he would have seen this target appear further from the coast than he was used to seeing aircraft appear. His subconscious indicated to him that something was wrong, even though he did not consciously recognise why.

Other studies have shown professionals in other areas getting a 'feel' for something without knowing the evidence. In the medical profession, midwives can develop a skill in spotting certain conditions for newborn babies, and paramedics learn to spot signs of heart attacks, even in people who haven't yet had any clear symptoms themselves (and can be months away from an actual attack). These paramedics also often describe themselves as having ESP. What they are actually doing is just making subconscious connections between someone they are seeing and the experience they have had with patients over many years.

It can be useful to examine some of the situations where Klein believes that conscious (he calls it 'rational') decisions will be made. These are where you:

- Need to justify your decision

- Are resolving conflict

- Need to find an 'optimised' solution

These can be contrasted with where the subconscious dominates (recognition-primed) decisions. In a social engineering context, these are where your target:

- Is under time pressure

- Has ill-defined goals

- Is in a dynamic situation

Clearly, when faced with a social engineering attack, the above conditions could easily apply. It is very unlikely that the target will be highly experienced in the situation.

A common belief is that it takes about 10 years in a given field to develop the skills to be classed as an 'expert'. Some people express it as 10,000 hours directly engaged in an activity. This is likely to be the point where an individual has enough experience for their subconscious to be able to direct them accurately when they cannot see answers consciously. You can spot people who have this level of expertise – they are extremely relaxed, but very capable. They see things with an expert eye and associated understanding.

A final example from Klein's work nicely illustrates the conditions of developing real expertise. In 1981, Klein ran a test of whether people could identify, from a selection of videos, who was experienced in conducting cardiopulmonary resuscitation (CPR). All the videos showed people doing CPR who had just completed the necessary training. However, one of them showed an experienced paramedic doing the same.

Klein showed the videos to three groups:

1. Beginners who had just completed the same training.

2. Instructors in CPR techniques

3. Experienced paramedics who had used CPR on many occasions.

As expected, the paramedics easily spotted the expert from the videos.

The beginners were also very good at spotting the skilled and experienced CPR delivery. However, the instructors were quite bad at spotting the expert. Although the instructors had knowledge, their direct experience did not involved real situations, or seeing experts deliver CPR – all of their experience was working with beginners.

This reminds me of the experiment I once heard of where a group of psychology students were placed inside a mental institution, pretending to be mentally ill. The experiment didn't last very long, as it was decided that it was too dangerous, following signs that the 'actors' were actually becoming mentally ill themselves.

However, one interesting fact emerged following the experiment. When the staff at the mental institution were asked to identify who had been acting as mentally ill, they found it almost impossible. However, when asked, the other patients had no difficulty in telling who were the imposters. This is another demonstration of where so-called experts can have quite limited experience and real expertise.

Target Selection

The immediate reaction of a social engineering target is an interesting factor in potential choice of target. Previously, I have described targeting people who look experienced in their role, as they will often have developed an automatic approach to the job, with their subconscious taking over the activity. This can lead to them being easier to misdirect and manipulate.

I used this, as explained in *Hacking the Human I*, when targeting railway inspectors to trick them into thinking my standard class rail ticket was first class. Their experience meant they were performing the activity with little conscious thought, so my manipulation of their subconscious was sufficient.

Sometimes, though, I might use the converse logic, and target someone who appears to be new to a role. In this case, I am not wanting the experienced person to get that 'gut feeling' that something is unusual with the situation. Here, I am looking to cause an element of confusion, where their subconscious doesn't have an immediate answer. I also combine this with applying some pressure, so that they cannot consciously evaluate the situation. In this scenario, prompting the subconscious helps them in coming to the right decision to help me in my social engineering attack.

Are They A Threat?

Where intuition is also particularly fascinating is where we get an immediate feeling about an individual. This is of particular interest to the social engineer, as our target will be making immediate judgments about us from the moment we interact with them.

It is useful to start to listen more to your immediate (and subconscious) reactions to people.

From an evolutionary point of view, the ability to judge friend or foe is a valuable advantage. You make many assessments of people based on their dress, appearance, and communication (verbal and non-verbal). The accuracy of your initial impressions will, however, depend upon a number of factors:

1. Does this person remind you of someone else (consciously or subconsciously)? If so, you will quickly allow them to inherit the history of the person you associate them with.

2. Does your depth and breadth of experience in human interactions give you enough subconscious experience to make snap judgments?

As a social engineer, I use the fact that people make quick judgments about individuals that they meet to my advantage. "He didn't look like a threat" is a typical comment made by people who have allowed me access to facilities. My dress and actions do not conform to their perception as to what a threat would look like.

In researching this area, I recently came across an interesting book, *Simple Heuristics That Make Us Smart* (Oxford, 1999). I was drawn to a chapter by Goldstein and Gigerenzer with the great title, "How Ignorance Makes Us Smart".

This has some interesting observations on the subconscious ability to recognise things from the past, even where the conscious brain cannot articulate where the memory comes from. Particularly interesting is the example of research showing our ability to recognise faces from pictures seen the day before. A high rate of correct identification was achieved even with a total number of images being 10,000 (the subjects chose 8,300 correctly).

This demonstrates a great subconscious ability to identify faces, which is not entirely surprising, given the evolutionary advantage of recognising friend from foe.

The subconscious is clearly of critical importance to us, and we now need to explore its working in more detail. Why not start with a situation where the conscious brain appears not to be engaged at all?

I Had A Dream

It is 6:10 a.m., and I have just woken up from an interesting dream. I am writing this immediately whilst my recollection is still quite fresh.

The scenario was as follows:

1. A large company had just had a major IT failure.

2. I had been brought in to troubleshoot the scenario, and sort out the mess. This was not to fix the IT system (this had already been done), but to find out the root cause of the problem that had led to the issue occurring.

Now, my personal theory of dreams is quite straightforward: your conscious brain shuts down and your subconscious plays with recent events and memories. As your subconscious doesn't understand logic, crazy things happen.

However, this dream stuck in my memory, as it contained various elements of logic:

1. I immediately sacked the six people who turned up late. For the purposes of the review, this established my authority and obtained the attention of the remaining people. It was a rather dramatic way to establish my authority, but has some logic to it.

2. A table I was leaning against collapsed, which is a simple case of applying the laws of physics.

3. Everyone looked quite down and depressed – quite logical, given the circumstances.

4. I acknowledged someone I knew, but the expression on his face told me he didn't want our knowing each other to be known to the group. This was a logical way for him to be acting in the circumstances, given that I was there to 'shake things up' somewhat.

5. I presented the team with two very logical questions: Firstly, was the team generally pretty good, not perfect by any means, but up to the job? and the incident just a case of 'shit happens'? Or, were the team, systems and the whole operation just plain 'in the shit' continually?

Each of the above contains a certain amount of logic – the sort of thing my conscious brain is good at coming up with on the spot. So was my conscious brain playing a role?

A factor that we might need to consider is how much of this logic was learned. Was the subconscious simply playing out a scenario (or multiple scenarios) that it had seen in action, including the elements of what looked like my conscious and logical behaviour? After all, dreams are not completely crazy and illogical; just elements of them are.

However, the logical I observed wasn't quite as logical as it might have been with a fully functioning conscious brain in operation. For example:

Was sacking part of the team a good idea? They might have been the best people, who could contribute the most. They might have had a very valid reason for being late. The effect on the others might have been very negative, and more damaging to the objectives I had than the benefits of establishing my authority (after all, was this really necessary in this situation)?

So, with a little reflection, my actions would have been tempered. I had clearly overreacted – you could say letting my emotions (subconscious) rule.

In my case, this dream had various links to my personal experience.

1. The people were Scottish. This links to two recent events. A client of ours in Scotland has just lost virtually all of its IT team. The IT director left, and the majority of his long-standing team left to join him over the next few months. Not surprising, as he was first rate at his job, and his team were similarly impressive. They had been a pleasure to work with. This development had left me concerned about the client's ability to maintain anything like their previous level of IT (and security) management. Also, as I write the news is currently covering a major incident at a Scottish bank, where an IT

failure has led to days of disruption to account holders. Last night, I watched a news interview with a 'banking systems expert', who came out with extraordinary waffle – and the interviewer took it all in.

2. I have been brought into situations like this by some of our clients. It has nothing to do with information security (unless you apply the broader definition of security including 'availability' of information). This is more where a CTO has used our services and respects our ability to get to the heart of complex issues and present them in plain English. My most recent example was a major retailer that had managed to bring its whole UK network of stores down, following what should have been a piece of routine maintenance.

3. The setting was more of a classroom environment. As I have a background in teaching and training, this was again, to some extent, a familiar re-run of my experiences.

Thus, it appears the dream was a compilation of recent events and previous experience, with the illusion of logic being a re-run of observed logic.

This makes me think of the concept of 'lucid dreams' – the ability of the conscious brain to recognise a dream and play a part. However, is this just re-running ideas that have been consciously thought about by the waking, conscious brain? How much is the conscious brain actually in charge of the dream, given the relatively low level of control that it has even when we are awake?

It does appear that the subconscious constructs the dream from stored memories, and adds some (subconscious) creativity.

My second example is another dream that I made notes from, having been woken mid-dream.

I was walking down a road I recognised near where I grew up, to get into my car. I found my grey BMW 7 series, and got in, and then pressed the key to unlock the car (even though I was already inside).

The key locked the car, started the engine, locked the steering, and set off.

I realised it wasn't my car.

The car increased speed and spun so that it was now going backwards, down quite a steep hill, past lots of parked cars, lampposts, buildings, and people jumping out of the way.

These people included an old man using a zimmer frame (I pressed the horn repeatedly to warn him, and he dived away at the last minute). I knew there was going to be a major impact at some stage, so I climbed onto the back seat to protect myself.

I kept looking up to see where I was, and then dropped back to lying on the rear seat with my back pressed against the bench seat awaiting the impact – still nothing! I looked up again to see that the car appeared to be keeping within the confines of the road. The car appeared to be deflecting off walls and lampposts, even though I was not feeling any impacts.

I saw a major road approaching, and recognised the potential to be hit by passing traffic as I crossed this road. I moved briefly back into the front, to engage the flashing hazard warning lights. I was hoping that someone would see these. Then I went back and resumed my position lying on the back seat.

Still no impact!

I adjusted my position, making sure my back was flat against the rear seat, and my head was also pressed back, waiting for the impact. Still nothing!

I looked up, and found myself amongst new streets, then a field, then another street – still with no collisions.

Finally, I came to a halt at the far end of a field filled with a group of young army cadets, who came over to see what had happened with this car.

I asked them to get whoever was in charge, and they brought over an elderly chap with a beard.

I asked him to call the police.

I got out of the car. It was now yellow, and an earlier model of the

BMW 7 series - I should have known it wasn't mine.

I then saw a petrol station and recognised that I was glad I missed that, as the resulting explosion would surely have killed me!

Then I went and bought some chocolate, saying to the person selling it to me that it is the best thing for dealing with going into shock.

I then placed a call to the police, explaining what had happened. I started with, "You aren't going to believe this."

Finally, I telephoned a journalist from a daily BBC radio news show, and offered him the story, saying that I preferred he write this, rather than let the tabloid press get it wrong.

I then heard a (somewhat strange) sounding police siren, only to then find this was my morning alarm call in the hotel.

It was quite an adventure, so it was interesting to think about where my subconscious found all this:

1. I drove three BMW 7 series cars for more than 10 years – one was grey (or light blue).

2. I do rather like yellow (sports) cars.

3. I reviewed an ECSC student job application late last night – he was an army cadet. This drew my attention, particularly as it didn't fit with the personality I was constructing from the rest of the letter and CV.

4. A few days before, I had watched an early edition of Top Gear, with Lewis Hamilton, the Formula 1 racing driver, describing a 180 mile-per-hour crash where he had time to think as he flew through the air (backwards) and braced himself against the back of his seat. As time slows down in situations like this, he had time to plan for the impact and, he said, 'quite enjoyed' the experience.

5. I regularly listen to the journalist that I had phoned when on my hotel travels within the UK.

6. The tabloid press are in the news at the moment as I write this, with charges being brought against various journalists for mobile telephone 'hacking' – listening to people's voicemail because they hadn't set any security. It was a stupid system offered by the telephone companies using default PINs, putting efficiency and cost before security.

7. I know that sugar helps deal with trauma and associated shock. I was told this over dinner with a bunch of ex-SAS soldiers. I was taking part in a 'morning raid' for a business in Africa. No, I wasn't there to shoot guns, or put people into hypnosis. Actually, I was doing a forensic analysis of computers that were being seized as part of a raid connected with the identification of internal fraud within a multinational company.

So there were quite a few elements of the dream that were based on my own experiences, some very recent.

It was also interesting to look at the apparent logic that I was applying to what appeared to be quite an illogical set of circumstances, where I:

*   Pressed the horn to warn pedestrians.

*   Climbed onto the back seat to prepare for impact (even though the front may well have been better).

*   Adjusted my position, to keep my head and back in contact with the seat.

*   Engaged hazard warning lights.

*   Called the police.

I would suggest that if I had been consciously processing this logic, then I would have also recognised the dream at the time. Therefore, these must all be 'learned' logic, with the conscious brain still shut down. By this, I mean that these responses give the illusion of logic, but are actually based on previous experience and learning – they are not logic that has been consciously constructed from the circumstances in which I found myself.

Did I work anything out consciously, or just apply learned behaviours to the situation?

Based on these examples, it is my conclusion that dreams are an illustration originating in the subconscious when it is freed from the intervention of the conscious brain. As the subconscious is given free reign, without the constraints of feedback from the physical environment, it constructs a world based on previous experience.

Is dreaming unique to humans? My observation is that it is not. I have owned quite a few dogs in my life and, as other dog owners will verify, on occasion you can observe dogs dreaming. They move their legs with small movements in time with a running motion, and even can be heard giving small barks as they dream.

It is interesting to contrast dreams with hypnosis, as they both appear to indicate the conscious brain is disengaged, and the subconscious takes charge:

Dreaming – there is usually no physical interaction with the environment

Hypnosis – there is continued interaction with the physical environment.

Some people do contend that hypnosis is actually just freeing up the conscious brain to accept subconscious directed actions (as usual), but with an accepted belief that the hypnotist is directing these.

However, we have to be careful not to assume that the conscious brain has too much control even when it appears to be engaged'. As we shall see, our assumption that we are in charge when awake, and not under hypnosis, could just be the biggest illusion of all time.

The potential implications for trying to protect ourselves from social engineering attacks are huge. If we aren't in control of our actions, then how do we protect ourselves?

The Art Of Delusion

Do you really know why you make the decisions that you do? One of our sales team once decided he wanted to really understand why our clients were buying certain services from ECSC. He asked my opinion on the matter. I expressed great doubt on the value of spending time asking. My considered opinion was that either they wouldn't want to tell us why or they wouldn't actually understand why. In either case, the resulting data would be of little value.

Still, he set off for his first client meeting, determined to start his objective research.

A couple of hours later, he returned from the meeting, only to declare that perhaps I was correct. He asked the client why he had bought the solution he had in place, only to get the response, "Ian told me to". My colleague (wisely) decided that he was probably better just concentrating on sales, rather than research.

Now, I make a point of not using any psychological trickery in 'sales' situations – or at least not trying consciously to do so. Having said that, after years of study and practice, techniques do move into the subconscious and become somewhat automatic, as they did this morning, when I found myself automatically co-ordinating my breathing rate with a client during a routine discussion.

If you haven't read my previous title, or attended a presentation on the topic, this is a rather subtle – and quite effective – method to develop instant rapport with someone. It has the distinct advantage that it is not as easily detectable as the more obvious (and mainly misunderstood) body language matching techniques that you might have come across.

Asking someone why they took a particular decision is a little bit like asking someone who works for you why they are leaving your employment in favour of another. They either give you the answer they think you want to hear, or they try to rationalise what is actually a very irrational decision-making process. Mind you, it is worth trying to ask them to, on occasion, be able to observe the level of irrationality and delusion in the decision-making process.

Another good example of irrational behaviour is the watching of daytime television.

I am currently sitting in my hotel room, having just finished an evening of work, and am doing a final half hour on my book. I arrived quite early at my hotel, having finished my client work in London by mid-afternoon and with only 30 minutes to travel by train from the city centre.

On arriving, I thought I would take a break, as that morning had featured a 5:30 a.m. taxi pickup from home. So I switched on the television to see what delights daytime television had to offer. I have now discovered Deal or No Deal.

If you haven't seen this show, or some derivative, let me describe it briefly.

It appears that there are about 20 contestants, but only one has a chance of winning (I'm not quite sure why the others are so interested in proceedings). Each contestant has a sealed box, containing a label for an amount of money. These seem to range from 50 pence to 250,000 pounds sterling.

The single contestant 'playing' directs other contestants to open their boxes one by one, with lots of dialogue in between. As the different amounts are revealed, a large screen shows which amounts are left.

Apparently, at the end of the game, the player chooses between their sealed box and the one remaining with another contestant. They know the two amounts (still showing on the large screen) but don't know which is which. They win the amount they select.

It sounds very simple: a game of chance with selection based on zero knowledge. It is therefore an impossible game to 'play', as there cannot be any logical strategy. Exactly the same outcome could be achieved by simply selecting from two envelopes, each with a value of winnings inside (however, that would leave too long for the advertisements).

Interestingly, the host (and player, with contributions from the other 'contestants') appear to make this last a whole show.

I hope you are with me so far, and sorry if you are a fan (you will be more sorry when you read my analysis).

A further complication (it needed it) was that someone (called the 'banker') keeps calling the host, at certain intervals, on an old fashioned telephone to make the player an 'offer'. This offer is a cash amount for them to take, rather than proceeding with the game. They accept the offer ('deal') or decline it ('no deal') to play further, with a chance to win more (or end up with less than the offer).

The episode I saw (most of) had a schoolteacher, who had eight boxes remaining, with the large screen showing the following box values: £5, £50, £500, £3,000, £20,000, £35,000, £50,000, and £250,000. According to the host, she was 'doing very well' at this point.

The banker called, and offered her £22,000 to stop at that point.

Now if my calculation is correct, eight boxes with a total of £358,555 means that on average, a box will be worth £44,819.38. Therefore, £22,000 was a terrible offer and should be turned down.

Of course, you might not apply such simple logic, particularly as the young lady playing said that £22,000 was a "life changing" amount.

Anyway, she accepted the 'deal'. I thought this would be quite a happy ending. Unfortunately, the host then made her continue to play to see what she would have won, on the assumption that her choices would be the same. In the end, the poor young lady was left with £35,000 and £250,000 as the final two boxes. Her accepted £22,000 at this point looked more like a major disappointment.

Luckily, from the final two boxes, she picked the £35,000, so she didn't feel too bad having not turned down £250,000 for only £22,000.

In this largely mindless game, something very interesting was happening. The choice of the £22,000 deal against a position worth £44,819.38 didn't bother me. The logic is quite sound: a relatively large amount guaranteed is better than only a chance of a bigger sum. Even if the odds say you are likely to get a bigger sum are in your favour, a risk of only £5 would likely lead to the logical conclusion to accept the 'deal'.

Actually, the game is somewhat based on what is known as Allais' Paradox. Maurice Allais was a Nobel Prize winner who, prior to receiving his prize, presented a question to a meeting of economists looking at risk. At a simple level, he asked whether you would prefer different amounts with different chances of being awarded them. The interesting finding was that if a figure had a 100% chance of success, then it appeared to get a far greater weighting compared with the other options. For example, if I offer you a:

1. 50% chance of £100, or

2. 25% chance of £200

then you should, in theory, find each equally attractive.

The amounts are not too dissimilar (or particularly life-changing), and the odds work out the same. Overall, you can expect a £50 return.

However, if the choice is:

1. 100% chance of £500,000, or

2. 90% chance of £600,000

then you find that the vast majority of people will select the first option, even though the odds are in favour of the second (on average, you will receive £540,000 with option 2).

This finding has challenged the thinking of decision theorists. These are a select group of eminent thinkers who are destined to be disappointed with the illogical nature of the human brain.

Personally, based on my own studies and observations during my work, I find this choice to be entirely predictable. People don't like a loss. The prospect of winning money, but critically with a chance of not winning it, will invoke the feeling of potential loss. It is similar to the disappointment some athletes show when they win a silver medal in the Olympic Games. They have just come second out of the population of the Earth in a given event. Wow! Even coming 53rd should (at a logical level) be reason to celebrate. However, they haven't 'won' second place. Instead, they feel they have 'lost' first place. Other athletes, who didn't perceive a chance of winning gold, would be delighted with the gain of silver.

Therefore, the 90% chance of £600,000 presents the chance of not gaining anything. For most people, the 'loss' would be significant.

So it wasn't this decision process that I found interesting with *Deal or No Deal*. Rather, it was the interaction between the host, player and other contestants during the rest of the game – specifically, during the selection of which box to open next.

With absolutely no information as to which box had which sum, all you could do was pick at random. However, each box was been held by a contestant, and was numbered (1, 2, 3, etc). Somehow, everyone appeared to have completely bought into the concept that this game could be played, with strategy and tactics. Quotes included:

"The boxes are being kind",

"Are you feeling lucky?",

"Is it going to be kind for you?", and

"The boxes are recognising your courage" (I really like this one!)

Opening (and therefore rejecting) low amounts meant hugs and kisses. Choices were being made of feelings, lucky numbers, etc.

The player used tactics such as:

"I knew I would open box 10 at this point – that is my birth date", or

"Three is the age of my daughter, I'm leaving that one for later".

Some choices also seemed to be linked to the contestant standing behind the box, who opens it when chosen.

"I will now ask Simon – I have felt a special connection to him today."

Overall, the situation is a classic mass delusion: a game of pure chance, nothing more than random selection, turned into a relatively, and seemingly infinitely variable, complex set of strategic and tactical 'choices'.

I now want to play, simply to test whether I could use cold logic and calculation without getting sucked into the craziness.

Why have we evolved to a state of such delusion?

Is it simply a lack of education in the field of mathematics and calculating chance?

After some thought, with the starting point that evolution tends to make smart choices, I have decided that this delusion is related to our human ability to extract meaning. If you think about human history, we have developed our environment through our ability to add structure and meaning to what we observe:

- In ancient times, people attributed meaning to supernatural beings.

- Now, we (mostly) leave this to scientists – and they find meaning through the development of hypothesis, and test this with experiment, subject to peer review.

Personally, I prefer the scientific approach – "we don't 'know' – but this theory is the best we have, based on available data", rather than the ancient 'belief/faith' approach.

I don't intend to get all 'anti-religion' at this point. Others have written more eloquently on the subject, and I don't wish to alienate readers that will be having enough trouble reading and objectively evaluating my understanding of the human brain and aligning it with their religious convictions.

I have 'faith' in the fact that progress is made when humans use observation, analysis (and some creativity) to find meaning and explanation in their surroundings. And, importantly, stay open to new ideas, when these have the potential to be better than previous theories.

So, what is happening with this television game, and the almost extreme delusion?

Clearly, meaning is being attached wherever possible to what are specifically designed to be truly random events. You would be very challenged to come up with a better experiment to illustrate the human tendency for delusion. (I wonder if they sell a box set of the series?)

This belief in some meaning to the outcomes of the game leads to the development of strategy and tactics. Every twist and turn leads to adaption of the belief to fit the data.

Therefore, in one round of box opening, we get the observations that:

"The boxes are being kind to you today, and your strategy is paying off." The audience is being whipped up into almost a frenzy of excitement as low value boxes are opened, leaving more high value ones.

I wasn't quite sure what the strategy was – selecting people (and boxes) based on random pieces of information was stretching the definition of 'strategy' somewhat.

Then, moments later, we have:

"It's amazing how the game can turn against you, despite your bravery."

The audience are now shocked at the latest turn of events, feeling sorry for the poor contestant.

At this point, I am shouting, "RANDOM CHANCE!" at the television.

To reinforce his 'bad boy' role, the banker revises his latest offer downwards, exaggerating the effect of the downturn in luck. Although the player hasn't actually won or lost anything yet, they feel that they have just lost, as the previous deal is now not available.

Of course, we know people make illogical choices with money – that's why they buy lottery tickets. A lottery is bad on a number of levels. As well as being a clear tax on the poor (who are more likely to play), it also sets an expectation that achieving desirable outcomes in your life is more about chance than through hard work. Just think of all the books they could buy with the money they spend on the lottery – a much more reliable way to success in your life.

Having said that, you clearly don't need to be told the value of reading, as evident by your interaction with this publication.

I think the National Lottery slogan should have to be, "the more you play, the more you lose."

Actually, even better would be to accompany adverts for lotteries with the findings of research that shows that, in the medium to long term, jackpot winners are less happy than those that weren't 'lucky' enough to win.

Another great example of irrational decision-making, supported by high levels of delusion, is that of trying to predict the stock market, which is a massive money making industry, charging people to manage their investment portfolios. However, research clearly shows that fund managers are no more skilled than 'lucky' – and charge higher fees. There has been no evidence found that past performance has any correlation to future success, proving that the whole industry adds no value.

However, not only do the individuals who buy such services believe in their value, but (most of) those in the industry also believe that they add value. The state of delusion dominates – people see patterns and believe that positive results must be linked to their skill.

Borges, Goldstein, Ortmann, and Gigerenzer tested a great theory in their paper "Can Ignorance Beat the Stock Market?" Basically, they decided to see if the strategy of making investment decisions purely on recognition of company name would give positive results. They called this an 'ignorance-based investment decision'.

Now, before you let your subconscious decide to invest your life savings based on one single study, I must transmit some warning signals to your decision-making cortex. Firstly, the experiment was conducted in a bull market, where most stocks were rising. Secondly, the study only lasted six months. Any 'expert' will tell you that investing in stocks and shares should be regarded as a long-term investment (mind you, they often tell you that after their investment advice turns out to be poor in the short to medium term).

The choice of people to make the investment decisions was quite important – they couldn't be experts, as they would recognise all the companies on the stock exchange. Equally, they couldn't be completely ignorant of the companies – they had to have some knowledge so that they could select based on some level of recognition.

The headline results were impressive for a six-month 'investment':

a 47% gain for the 'recognised' portfolio.

A selection based on the opposite quality of companies that none of the selecting group recognised produced a gain of only 13%.

Across a number of tests, the gains for the selection based on recognition consistently beat the market index, fund managers and randomly selected stocks and shares.

It is also worth noting that the gains measured did not take into account that for fund managers, you have to also deduct management fees that can run into quite a large percentage of your invested fund. This makes the results above even more impressive.

Another area of delusion that gives us insight into the process of developing beliefs is that of conspiracy theories. I enjoy reading and watching conspiracy theories. Although I treat each one with a healthy dose of scepticism, they can still be great fun.

My underlying observation (and therefore criticism), regarding conspiracies is that they assume a level of competence at an organisational, military, and political leadership level that does not exist. I remember, in my early managerial days, working in an organisation where employees had a wide range of conspiratorial explanations for the strange decisions of management.

As I myself progressed to senior management level, I quickly discovered that these decisions were more due to dysfunctional processes. The decisions were difficult to understand for most employees, and exacerbated by poor communication by managers. So, in an absence of explanation, theories emerged of underlying motives.

Since, in my later career, I have had the opportunity to work with government, multinational corporations and the military, I can confirm that the competence required to carry out most conspiracies is somewhat lacking.

It is understandable that people look for explanations to perceived puzzles. They take comfort from the belief that someone is in control and directing their lives.

If, for a moment, you accept that the subconscious is indeed in control, then the conscious brain must be in a constant state of delusion regarding its own decision-making. Therefore, we all have a well-developed ability to create similar delusional beliefs. This ability to create a theory to explain an observation is a great evolutionary asset. Scientific development is the positive outcome of this ability.

Of the conspiracy theories that prefer, I tend to pick those that are the most outlandish in nature. If a conspiracy is quite likely to be true (and therefore quite rational and logical), then it loses its appeal for study.

For example, faking the moon landings is a wonderful conspiracy, mainly due to the vast number of people that would have to be involved to pull it off.

I recently saw another grand conspirator re-emerge into more public view – David Icke. Icke is a fascinating character, having started his career as a footballer, then a television sports presenter. He then made a switch into politics, and (largely due to his abilities in front of the camera) quickly emerged as one of the leaders of the UK Green Party. However, he was quickly removed from this position when he started to make public statements that appeared more prophet-like than political.

This culminated in a rather (in)famous appearance on the UK's number one chat show in 1991, where he was interviewed by Terry Wogan. At the time (with only a small number of available television channels), this show was being watched by approximately one quarter of the UK's population.

By the time of the interview, Icke had declared himself the Son of God, and insisted on only ever wearing a purple track suit. As you might expect, he was ridiculed, and became a national joke.

However, Icke didn't go away. Rather, he continued to write, and present, and develop his theories.

After all this time, what has emerged is a rather ambitious conspiracy – namely, that the earth is being run by large lizards. These lizards are hidden from view by using shape-changing to hide in human form. Large numbers of historic leaders (past and present) are therefore actually lizards in disguise. Their numbers include the current queen.

Even my republican leanings don't quite stretch to the extent of thinking of the royal family as lizards.

These reptilian humanoid creatures apparently come from a specific stellar location – the Alpha Draconis star system (somewhere near the North Star, if you want to take a look) and, in addition to hiding in human form, live in underground bases.

This has all the hallmarks of a classic conspiracy theory: a bit crazy (to say the least), but also vast in scale, and able to encompass a large number of individuals and events.

As you might expect in a global conspiracy, Icke has much 'research' to support his theory. He creates quite compelling threads of dialogue linking a vast array of historical 'facts', and blames many of the current challenges that society faces on his theory. This creates a rather attractive proposition for someone feeling powerless in a global society, where power appears distant.

In observing Icke, I have no doubt that he is genuine. He really believes his own story, and is persuading himself as much as his followers.

Icke now has many books, and presents to sell-out crowds for up to six hours at a time.

I set aside some time recently to watch a few of his online videos, particularly to see how he explains, and rationalises his belief. It was interesting to watch him take snippets of scientific fact/theory and link them to his own overarching belief. It was a similar process to that repeated by religious leaders: as facts emerged that threaten ancient writings, they managed to turn them into supporting evidence. Where this is impossible, they simply changed previously factual writings into metaphor or proverbs.

In one speech, Icke took two scientific facts/theories:

- Firstly, the human eye only uses a small amount of the available electromagnetic spectrum to evolve sight.

- Secondly, scientists use the term 'dark matter' when referring to the need for more matter to exist in the universe than we can currently observe or detect. This additional matter is required to support the current mathematical models of our universe.

Icke manages to link these to proof that shape-changing lizards exist. He explains that the reason we don't 'see' the lizards is that they can operate within other frequencies to those we can see. This is taking a rather limited understanding of electromagnetic radiation, but rather neatly uses the "we can't see everything" to explain lizards hidden from sight.

I am not sure why this is necessary, as the shape-changing nature of the lizards would appear to fully account for their ability to hide from view.

However, David went further, explaining that dark matter accounts for the majority of the universe. He then points out that if lizards can evolve into the wide range of creatures that we can see, within the matter we can observe, then why can't they also evolve beyond this point within the dark matter that we cannot see?

By this point, physicists will likely be either screaming and shouting at the screen, or just shaking their heads in disbelief.

This extreme shaping (pardon the pun) of science to fit belief is a great example of delusion.

Whilst examining more extreme conspiracy theorists can be good fun, it also gives you insight into just how easily we can be deluded into believing the cause of an observation.

Let's Experiment

I recently came across some interesting research that illustrated the delusion of the conscious brain quite nicely.

Lewicki, Hill, and Bizot conducted some research that involved participants viewing a screen split into quadrants. A letter X appears in one of the quadrants and the participant has to press one of four buttons –

one corresponding to each quadrant.

At one level, this is just a case of measuring response times. However, the researchers introduced a level of pattern to the appearance of the Xs on screen. This pattern was quite complex, but did exist. The participants found that their performance steadily improved, compared with when the appearance was random.

The performance increase was confirmed not to be just an increase in reaction times, since, when the pattern was changed back to random selection, the participants' performance dropped back to the previous level.

So, the participants had identified the pattern and changed their behaviour accordingly.

The surprising finding was that, due to the complexity of the pattern, the participants did not consciously recognise that they had identified any pattern. They did not know why their performance had improved, and then gone back.

This demonstrates a subconscious process of learning, and resulting change of behaviour, with the conscious brain being apparently out of the loop.

The experiment then gets even more interesting, as the participants were asked to explain the changes in their performance through the activity.

Excuses included people saying they had "suddenly lost the rhythm" in their fingers, and others that insisting the experimenters must have done something to distract them. Some guessed the screen was flashing 'subliminal' images or messages to distract them. This was not the case.

A final surprising aspect of this experiment was that the participants were actually psychology professors. Despite knowing that the experiment was concerned with subconscious process, they still continued to invent excuses in order to rationalise their own behaviour.

With such a divide between our own perception of being in control and the reality, as exposed by recent experiments, it would appear that the social engineer is always going to have rich pickings when targeting people for information.

So, if the conscious brain isn't really in charge, what is it that leads to the brain making decisions?

Let Battle Commence

Understanding your conscious brain, and its relationship to your subconscious is vital in our exploration of the mind.

I have tried to negotiate with my subconscious. It doesn't respond as I would like. I just can't reason with it! A psychologist might use the term 'executive control' to describe the control that the conscious mind has over the subconscious. However, there are many cases where the conscious brain appears not to be able to control what the subconscious does.

What do you conclude when someone doesn't follow your instructions?

It could be that they aren't listening, or refusing to comply, or perhaps they aren't intelligent enough to understand?

Through my social engineering, I began to wonder if I was attributing too much 'intelligence' to the subconscious. Anthony Greenwald is a social psychologist who has come to the conclusion that the subconscious is much less clever than that imagined by Freud and his contemporaries.

This led me to start thinking about the subconscious as a large number of relatively 'dumb' processes that still hold the power.

Let's take the three examples previously discussed that illustrate where behaviour confirms the power of the subconscious. These are good examples of major problems in the western world, and examples of behaviours that more 'advanced' countries are currently exporting to developing countries. The three behaviours that illustrate a similar effect are:

1. Eating too much, despite knowing that it is having a negative effect on your health.

2. Smoking, even when you know it will shorten your life by 10 years

3. Excess consumption of alcohol even after recognising the negative

effects on your life.

Let's for a moment imagine that you have two brains:

- Subconscious – works on feelings, likes and dislikes based on past experience.

- Conscious – applies 'intelligence' and logic to the situation.

The above behaviours have a common thread:

- Subconscious brain likes them. It associates each with pleasure:

    - Eating too much is very much built into our natural behaviour, from many generations of food scarcity. However, we make this worse by rewarding young people with high calorie foods as treats. We also brand some very unhealthy foods by referring to them as 'happy meals'.
    - Smoking usually starts with trying to be like your friends or acting like a grown-up – necessary, as the initial experience is quite unpleasant. Then the physical effects of dependency take effect, giving the illusion of pleasure (it is actually the removal of the negative effects of withdrawal, similar to caffeine).
    - Alcohol clearly has a physical effect that can be regarded as pleasurable (especially if you are the subconscious, which doesn't make the logical link to the hangover the next day). Interestingly, as with smoking, the first experience of alcohol is rarely a pleasure. We build a set of associations to pleasure over a period of time – for example, by consuming alcohol in situations of pleasure, such as weekends, holidays, and nights out with friends. This re-enforces to the subconscious the pleasure, without the negative side.

- Conscious brain knows they are bad, and understands the logical connection between them and long-term negative consequences.

So why, for so many people, does the subconscious win the battle?

These are great examples of where the subconscious is clearly in charge. People 'want' to change, but cannot seem to achieve this – even though they believe at a conscious level that they want to. Why can't someone do what they want? Is it not possible for the conscious brain make a decision and the subconscious falls into line? Just who is in charge?

More and more research is pointing to the possibility that the conscious brain does not actually make decisions. Rather, it accepts decisions from the subconscious and then is deluded into thinking that it has made that decision.

You can get a fascinating example of this by asking someone with one of the three addictions above to justify their continued use. Their language gives you clues as to their underlying beliefs and the justification that they 'invent' to help explain their actions to themselves.

Sometimes, they present a quite logical (to them) argument. For example, one of my friends who drinks rather too much and too often, has a rather well rehearsed argument that health guidelines on daily drinking levels have changed over time, and therefore the experts don't know what they are talking about.

The reality is that as the dangers of alcohol are better understood, the health advice evolves. So, for example, in the UK, there has recently been a change to say that in addition to having a safe daily limit to alcohol intake, you should also have two alcohol-free days per week.

The logic of rejecting the health advice because it has changed is a little bit like saying cigarettes must be good for you, because many years ago doctors used to recommend smoking to help certain medical conditions (isn't progress great?)

If you observe carefully, you can spot where a belief system predominates thinking. For example, a rather large friend of mine commented (as we were about 30 minutes late for lunch) that we should go and eat, "before we starve!" I looked at him, and my own 10kg overweight physique at the time, and (having seen the breakfast we had eaten merely three hours earlier) thought that starvation was somewhat unlikely in the near future.

These individuals (like all of us, to a certain extent) are being led by their subconscious automated behaviour. They are consciously constructing an argument and justification for their behaviour, as they cannot accept that they are not in control of their own bodies.

Let's accept that the subconscious is clearly quite powerful, and can be difficult to get it to 'change its mind'. Why is this so?

I would like us to consider some processes, and their level of automation, that can be correlated to subconscious control.

Let's go to the heart of the human body – quite literally. Like me, you won't have any direct control over its beating. It started early in your development in the womb and will continue (hopefully without much interruption) until you die.

Interestingly, my own heart stops regularly. Actually, it is more like a reboot than a stop, and apparently everyone's heart does this at least once a day. Anyway, a few years ago, mine was doing this every 10 beats or so.

What happens is that something goes wrong, and your heart has an inbuilt correction mechanism. Basically, it stops, and then starts afresh with a new beat cycle. As it has stopped for one beat, your blood (that is still circulating) fills up your heart and then when the next beat comes along, you feel a bit of thump as it empties the build up of blood.

My cure was quite simple: I stopped drinking copious amounts of caffeine. Alcohol doesn't help, either, but is not as bad as caffeine. (Although you might question my logic as my own justification for still partaking of the latter on occasion).

Anyway, back to the control. My guess is that like me, you have absolutely no direct control over your heartbeat. What you can do is to control it indirectly – if you sense danger, then adrenalin will speed it up, and conversely, if you relax deeply, you can slow it down somewhat.

Clearly, the overall beating is outside of our conscious control, and the individual actions of the parts of the heart work in sync (apart from mine on occasion).

Now stop breathing. That was quite easy. Please feel free to start again. Yes, breathe.

Breathing is clearly automatic, and subconsciously controlled. However, we can intervene and stop it (for a period of time – then the subconscious decides to overrule). I don't recommend trying this. Just take my word for it.

Not only can you stop your breathing, but you can also speed it up at will.

Let's move elsewhere in your body. I am currently sitting at my hotel desk typing. I can touch type, so this process is quite automated: I think of the words and my fingers largely work across the keys automatically. However, this isn't the same as my heart beating, as each individual hand and finger movement can also be stopped, started and redirected consciously. I can control every small movement if I want to, but also let automation take over. This is very much like my previously discussed guitar playing: each movement can be controlled, or it can be left to the subconscious with some conscious oversight and direction.

Running is a little like my typing, as I run when directed consciously. I don't have to think and direct every single individual muscle movement. Rather, I just consciously set the speed and direction and perhaps make corrections. My subconscious has long since learnt the process of running, even though I can control most of the muscles involved on an individual basis if required.

Other processes are only done consciously. I am sure you can think of a number of things that you only do when consciously directing yourself to. However, you will find that these are quite easily automated if you do them repeatedly – activities can move from fully and consciously controlled to being subconsciously controlled. This is a fundamental of our ability to learn skills, and a great evolutionary advantage.

Let's take these varying levels of conscious and subconscious control and organise them at four levels.

Human Processes

Level	Title	Description
4	Conscious	Only happens with direct, immediate conscious thought.

3	Directed	Activities we instruct, but made up of a number of interacting processes that can be automatic - e.g. running.
2	Semi-automatic	Largely automatic, but with conscious influence - e.g. breathing (can we stop it, or can we just block our throat and the automatic process pauses for a while before forcing us to resume?)
1	Automatic	Without any conscious interaction, e.g. food digestion, sneezing, heart beating (have some influence - indirectly), healing.

You could map each observed process (both conscious and subconscious) and activity under the four levels above.

My focus here is on actions and behaviours, and not memories. We all experience being able to recall something instantly, whereas other memories take longer, or may be impossible to retrieve. In my experience of social engineering, I am less concerned with the memory function of recall. I am more interested in the process of turning perceived knowledge into decisions and actions.

If we can see separate processes operating at different levels, what happens if we reject that the subconscious exists at all? By that, I don't mean a rejection of subconscious processes, but a contention that a single entity we might call the subconscious exists.

There are clearly subconscious processes. However, perhaps they are not part of a coherent whole. What if each of the individual processes we have explored above actually work in combination to give the illusion of a combined entity? This helps to explain why influencing the subconscious can be such a challenge – you are not dealing with a single entity, but a whole host of different mini 'subconsciae'.

Meeting Your Subconsciae

Therefore, I contend that a subconsciae controls your heart rate. It is completely ignorant of other processes, other than taking inputs from other subconsciae that it needs. Whilst I am not a medical professional,

I can guess that the heart needs to have input on your body's oxygen requirements. This same input likely also feeds into your breathing rate subconsciae. However, there will be no linkage between the subconsciae that helps me touch type and that which controls my heart rate, as there is no reason for extra oxygen as I type, given that my finger movements are quite modest.

These concepts helps explain why the subconscious is so difficult to control. Think of the term 'herding cats'. You can think of controlling the subconscious as more like influencing a diverse population, rather than directing an individual.

Let's think about the subconsciae that are controlling our friends with eating, smoking and drinking issues:

Eating is relatively simple to explain: a subconsciae knows that an empty stomach indicates that food supply has stopped. This triggers other subconsciae that make the sight, or smell, of food attractive. This is a very easily understood evolutionary advantage – most species are short of food, and filling the need is an important priority in everyday activity.

Smoking is a little more complex, as it is not a 'natural' process. There is very little evolutionary need to process vegetation, set fire to it, and breathe in the resulting fumes. You are more likely to start with subconsciae that tell you this is a bad thing, as particles entering your lungs are should generate an automated subconsciae response to tell you to stop the activity – this is why people don't generally like their first cigarette.

Because of this, tobacco pushers have to create a compelling reason for another subconsciae to overrule the sensible one that tells you that smoke is bad for your lungs. The most common reason that people articulate for their first encounter with smoking is peer pressure (direct or indirect). It is well understood that young people usually feel a strong need to conform with their peers.

Alcohol is similar to tobacco – its first consumption is rarely pleasurable, from a taste perspective. It requires concerted effort to get your subconsciae programmed to like it. As a subconsciae is not very smart, it doesn't link the negative consequences that follow drinking to the drink itself – in other words, it remembers the feeling and associated environment with having a drink, but not the aftereffects. The relevant subconsciae learn to associate the taste and smell of alcohol with a string of pleasurable experiences.

The more I examined human behaviour, the more I realised that a model of the subconscious as a community of separate subconsciae made sense. Had I invented something here?

My experience tells me that it is quite rare that you come up with something that hasn't already been thought of by someone else. Truly original thought is quite rare.

I am reminded of the weekend when I discovered a new process of hiding data within other data so that it could not be detected (quite early in my career in information security). I came into work and explained it to some technical colleagues. They didn't look very impressed.

"You don't understand", I said, "this really is important and will revolutionise security!"

"I presume you haven't heard of steganography," they said.

"No".

"Well, you have just re-invented it."

No prizes for being second.

And, sure enough, my recent discovery of the subconsciae actually had a long history. I think the earliest indication might be Pierre Janet in 1889, with the 'dissociation theory', which says that the mind is divided into separate functions that do not have intercommunication. However, I am sure a more extensive search could trace similar ideas even earlier.

What gets really interesting is when you start thinking how these independent subconsciae might work together (or against each other) to formulate a decision – or in some cases, to lead to paralysis of the decision-making process.

As a social engineer, you will want to further understand the ways that decisions are taken, as this gives us routes to influence these decisions.

Democracy
Always Wins

So, if we accept that rather than one subconscious, we have many subconsciae, how do they reach decisions, and how do they interact with the conscious brain?

As we saw back when looking at hacking the cloud in Part One, glucose depletion can make the conscious less active and therefore subconscious-led decision more likely. Psychologists sometimes call this effect ego-depletion, and work in this area has been pioneered by Roy Baumeister.

Perhaps it isn't only a lack of glucose that leads to a weakening of the conscious brain. In what must be one of the most famous psychological experiments with children, Walter Mischel gave some four-year-olds an interesting challenge. They were given a choice:

1. Eat the single cookie in front of them, or

2. Look at this cookie for 15 minutes (with no obvious distractions) and then be rewarded with two cookies.

Assuming that the child likes cookies, this is a fantastic illustration of the power (or otherwise) of the conscious logical mind.

The logical mind can work out that two cookies is better than one, and that simply waiting will result in an extra reward.

However, the subconscious is simply screaming, "Eat the cookie!" The subconscious does not recognise the future benefits, or the logic involved in its identification. The subconscious is very much restricted to living in the here and now.

The experiment resulted in about 50% of the children resisting for the later reward. This shows a nice separation between the 'strong-willed' and the 'weak'.

However, what made the experiment really interesting is that Mischel didn't end there. He tracked the long-term outcomes for the two groups of children over the next 15 years, into young adulthood.

The long-term prospects for those that could resist turned out to be significantly better. They scored higher in the standard intelligence tests, and were less likely to be tempted into a life on drugs. The ability to resist the simple decisions of the subconscious appears to be a significant advantage in life.

Thinking of the subconscious as multiple subconsciae made me think if perhaps our conscious brain might also be split in some way. This led me to the work of Keith Stanovich, and his book *Reality and the Reflective Mind*, where he argues that there are two distinct processes in the conscious mind:

- Algorithmic – raw computing power to solve problems (traditional intelligence)

- Rationality – ability to make logic decisions (free from illogical bias)

Illogical Decision-Making

If the subconsciae are illogical, and yet have undue influence over the conscious brain, we would expect people to show undue influence from factors that they do not recognise consciously. There are in fact numerous examples of this:

Malcolm Gladwell shares some examples of this in his popular book *The Tipping Point*, summarising research that shows that individuals' life choices can be influenced (to a statistically significant level) by their own names.

So, if you are called Dennis, you are slightly more likely to end up being a dentist than if your name has no relation to the profession. Surprising, but proved in a number of scenarios.

Psychologists Gary Wells and Richard Petty found that people could be influenced in their decision-making by whether they were told to nod or shake their head during an experiment. Those nodding were more likely to agree with statements and those shaking their head were more likely to disagree. Rather than head movement following a decision, it can actually work the other way around and influence a decision.

It would appear that the subconsciae that control head nodding also work in reverse. Nodding your had also transmits a signal that positively affects the decision in hand.

It is clear that subconsciae won't always agree. There must be an element of democracy, perhaps with certain subconsciae carrying more weight.

Perhaps the illogicality of the subconscious is a direct consequence of it being an often-conflicting mixture of subconsciae input and argument.

Conflict in the Subconsciae

Can we observe people receiving conflicting subconsciae advice? Is this when someone says, "I can't make up my mind"? Are they receiving equally weighted opinion from more than one subconsciae and therefore haven't been given a clear decision to believe was their own?

You will also know that sometimes people 'freeze' when faced with a situation that confuses them. You sometimes hear the term 'like a rabbit in the headlights' to describe this position. The brain is thrown into a state of utter confusion by conflicting signals.

Interestingly, some aircraft autopilots recognise this condition. If their inputs are confused and conflicting (usually due to one of more malfunctioning sensors), the autopilot is designed to 'give up' and pass control back to the pilot. It is assumed that the pilot will bring some sense to the situation, and it makes passengers feel more at ease to know a human is in control.

Unfortunately, it is also widely known to aircraft builders that air travel would overall be safer without pilots, as more accidents are due to pilot error than system failures. A good example of this is the crash of an Air France flight.

In this case, an Airbus aircraft did indeed suffer from some malfunctioning sensors – in this case, it was the airspeed sensors. This was due to flying through particularly bad storms en route from South America to France. As designed, the autopilot gave up and passed control to the three pilots.

If the pilots had done nothing, and just maintained all the flight settings as left by the autopilot, then the plane would have continued safely. Unfortunately, the most inexperienced of the three pilots was in charge (the most experienced was on a sleep break).

As it turned out, the pilots made the wrong decisions as to which controls were telling the truth and which were faulty. The least experienced pilot 'decided' that he needed to climb, and without an accurate indication of speed he put the plane into a stall. Despite the stall alarm going off over 50 times, he persisted with the course of action as the plane dropped out of the sky. Even the arrival and late intervention of the captain, and most experienced pilot, was too late.

So imagine your conscious brain is a not particularly bright, inexperienced, and very slow-thinking pilot. The subconsciae are the masses of dials and readouts in the cockpit, giving their input and advice for the pilot to act upon. However, in the case of the human brain, it is in autopilot most of the time. The pilot believes he is in control, but this is largely an illusion.

I like the term that philosopher Daniel Dennett came up with to explain the role of the conscious brain. He termed it the 'press secretary' – meaning that it was a close observer of a decision-making process, but its role was to offer explanation (or spin.)

This, along with my thoughts on the subconsciae population, made me consider the following proposition for the role of the conscious brain:

Being Prime Minister

Imagine you are the leader of your country. For me, this would be prime minister.

Now, imagine that you have to follow the will of the people in every decision you take. You are completely controlled by the population.

In every decision that comes across your desk, your staff has already worked out the course of action that will please most of the people that vote you into office. You have no choice but to take the decisions that will please the most people.

You might believe that this is pretty close to reality for many democratically elected leaders. However, I would hope that at least some of their decisions are taken for what they believe is the long-term benefit of the country. By 'long-term', I mean something that will have no significant benefit before they are up for re-election, but is of longer term benefit.

Now, back to my scenario: if every single decision had to be carried out to agree with the majority view on that particular issue, I want you to consider the following questions:

1. Would you be successful?

2. Would you still be 'in charge' of the country?

3. Would you feel powerful?

I would suggest this scenario is analogous to the conscious brain. Decisions are predetermined. You, the 'leader', are an observer with a belief in your own power.

There are times when different advisers (subconsciae) have different ideas – however, these are usually sorted out before the decision comes to you for your 'ratification'.

It is our delusion with regard to our decisions that makes the life of the social engineer possible. The attacker has just realised that people can be easily tricked and, through appropriate techniques, made to perform actions or release information.

To generate the required action from the target, a social engineer has to go through two steps:

1. Generate the appropriate subconsciae majority support for the action.

2. Facilitate a conscious process that gives the target a viable excuse or reason for their action, so as to reduce the chance of detection.

Believe It Or Not?

CHAPTER

In *Hacking the Human*, I put forward the conjecture that we do not consciously make decisions. In this follow-up, my exploration of the latest research shows a growing body of opinion that this is indeed the case.

The implications for social engineering are quite profound, raising questions about what is possible in terms of protection, and certainly undermining an approach based solely on 'conscious' training.

In the original *Hacking the Human*, I questioned the value of training. This observation was based on my experience of turning training into vulnerabilities during testing projects. This was further illustrated during some of the adventures in Part One.

Part Two has added further weight to this argument, through examination of the role of the subconscious, as illustrated by some of the latest academic research.

You may have found some of the contents of this book a little unsettling. Discovering that you may not have free will to control your actions can be disturbing, to say the least.

Does this mean that we cannot hold individuals to account for their actions?

Without a free and conscious decision-making process, is your future set – a series of programmed actions accompanied by a deluded belief in self-control?

These are interesting questions for philosophers, and other 'free' thinkers. You might wish to start what might be an intense journey of discovery with a little light reading on the subject. I can recommend the little book *Free Will* by Sam Harris. Building upon the research that shows the illusion of free will, he explores some of the impact this may have on our society.

Personally, I quite like to 'believe' that I am responsible for my actions. Even if at a pure logical level I might doubt this belief, it still helps me. Do you want to resign your life to a passive acceptance of fate, with no attempt to influence yourself or your environment? It's not a good starting point for a happy and fulfilled life. Perhaps a little delusion in life is a good thing.

PUTTING YOUR SUBCONSCIOUS TO WORK!

As we near the end of this exploration of the mind, let's drift a little into self-help.

Hacking the Human took me just short of four years to complete. I had valid excuses (and an understanding publisher). I was developing ECSC, having founded it on little more than a credit card (actually, I had an impressive collection of credit card debts after the first couple of years). I was also combining my business development with a full-time client-facing consulting role. Work on the book had to be done by grabbing time in hotels, planes, and trains.

As I write this, I am yet again drafting text whilst travelling by train, still leading ECSC, and still doing a full-time consulting role. However, something has changed, as my latest word total tells me that I have just reached 50% of the total words in *Hacking the Human* in just 11 weeks. And these are 'finished' elements, already having gone through a proofing stage by a trusted critical friend – not just outline notes.

What has changed? Am I not as busy as before? Actually, far from it, as my work commitments are if anything more demanding than during the work on *Hacking the Human I*.

What I have done is finely tuned my work, at a conscious (organisational and planning) level, but also at a subconscious level. I direct my subconscious to work on activities in the background. This means that when I do 'make time' to write, it tends to be just a case of typing what are already well-developed threads.

How is this done?

At a simple level, just 'chunk' a problem into small tasks. By focusing on something a little bit at a time, you give your subconscious reminders about it, and then allow it to go away and work on it.

Many people find they are very productive and creative just before deadlines. This is partly the pressure on them, and the fact that they must work on the task, with no option to procrastinate any longer. However, another element is that if they have been thinking about the task for long enough, their subconscious will have solved the difficult bits already.

In the case of this book, I didn't have a target of completing 50% of the book in 11 weeks. Actually, I did, but this isn't what I focused on. What I focused on was 3,500 words per week, and more specifically, what I had to do each day.

At the time of writing, I am heading home on a train, knowing that I am about to exceed 3,500 words for this week (and it is only Thursday). A little self-congratulation has its place.

The best, and most simple, way to progress a large project is very simple – just do something to progress it every day.

If you wish to go deeper, self-hypnosis can help. This is quite easy to learn, and can be quite effective at training your own brain. You cannot go as deep as you would under hypnotherapy (as you would not be able to direct yourself consciously). However, it can still be good at conditioning yourself with new 'beliefs'.

One powerful way to get your subconscious to work is to think about a problem as you go to sleep. This needs some practice, as you don't want to keep yourself awake thinking about the problem.

The trick here is not to try and solve a problem, but just to tell yourself to think about it and to come up with ideas. You will then find that first thing in the morning is a very productive, and creative, time, when these ideas and solutions emerge from your subconscious.

Actually, I never intended to write a follow-up to the original *Hacking the Human*. If you are one of the many people who 'persuaded' me to do so, then well done – you clearly have some developing social engineering skills. However, your work is not done. I now look to you and others in the field of information security (and the wider study of human behaviour) to further this exploration.

In particular, I ask that information security academics spend more time engaged with their psychology colleagues - departmental barriers are there to be broken.

I think that I have done my part in this field. The first *Hacking the Human* has already been 'borrowed from' extensively in other publications, and this (even without acknowledgement) is a good thing.

For me, it is now time to move on to new challenges, so for social engineering, I feel that I am now best served by the words of that great 20th century thinker, Forrest Gump, "That's all I have to say about that."

What are your new beliefs?

It is late at night, and I am sitting working on another long flight, so I thought I would offer you a final thought:

If you are new to the underlying psychology, you might find some of the contents of this book a little difficult to accept. You may have started this journey with a passing interest in social engineering, and ended up not knowing who you really are.

So, I thought I would leave you with a quote from the novel *Straight Man* by Richard Russo (thanks to Timothy Wilson for this):

"The truth is, we never know for sure about ourselves ... Which is why we have spouses and children and parents and colleagues and friends, because someone has to know us better than we know ourselves."

I have been fortunate to have some special people in my life that know me better than I do. I hope you find the same happiness in your life.